Christmas

O
HOLY
NIGHT!

O HOLY NIGHT!

Timeless Meditations on Christmas

A. Jean Lesher, Editor

Saint Mary's Press
Christian Brothers Publications
Winona, Minnesota

To my mother, Merle Olson,
who first told me the story of the birth of Christ.

 Genuine recycled paper with 10% post-consumer waste.
Printed with soy-based ink.

The clip art on pages 9 and 137 is from *Clip Art for Year A,* by Steve
Erspamer, SM (Chicago: Liturgy Training Publications, 1992). Copyright ©
1992 by the Archdiocese of Chicago, 1800 North Hermitage Avenue,
Chicago, IL 60622-1101. 1-800-933-1800. Used with permission. All rights
reserved.

The clip art on page 35 is from *Clip Art for Year C,* by Steve Erspamer,
SM (Chicago: Liturgy Training Publications, 1994). Copyright © 1994 by
the Archdiocese of Chicago, 1800 North Hermitage Avenue, Chicago, IL
60622-1101. 1-800-933-1800. Used with permission. All rights reserved.

The art on page 81 is by Vicki Shuck.

The publishing team included Carl Koch, development editor; Laurie A.
Berg, copy editor; Lynn Dahdal, production editor and typesetter; Maurine
R. Twait, art director and cover designer; cover art, Tom Lowes; pre-press,
printing, and binding by the graphics division of Saint Mary's Press.

The acknowledgments continue on page 164.

Printed in the United States of America

Printing: 9 8 7 6 5 4 3 2 1

Year: 2006 05 04 03 02 01 00 99 98

ISBN 0-88489-534-3

Contents

Preface

The Christmas story has entranced the imagination of peoples for two millennia in every land where it is told or sung or recited or read. The basics are quite simple: a baby was born in the Middle East to a young woman named Mary in humble surroundings. Heavenly angels proclaimed that this infant was the long-expected Messiah, or Savior, of us all. And he grew up to become the Christ, the Risen One, who redeems the world.

For all of us who have walked in darkness, he is a great Light. As the prophet Isaiah predicted long before the birth of Jesus, his name will be called Wonderful Counselor, the Prince of Peace, the Mighty God, and of the increase of his government and of peace, there shall be no end.

Each year we celebrate this birth, this life, this hope, for we know that God can bring us out of darkness and enable us to experience peace.

The readings in this collection come from many ages and lands and peoples. Most of them present aspects of the Christmas story that have withstood the test of time. They have been preserved from generation to generation as something profoundly worthwhile, something precious to retain and savor. They say something we want us and our children—the next generation—to remember. A few are contemporary, presenting modern insights into the old, old story. They are examples of the ongoing efforts by people of faith to celebrate the mystery of God in Jesus for our time, one of much religious pluralism and unsettling social and technological changes.

These selections are meant to be inspiring, even thought provoking, and to lend themselves to meditating on their meaning for our life today at the end of one millennium and the beginning of another. They can help us refocus on what this holy season means as we are surrounded by a cacophony of entreaties to buy our way into well-being.

The parts of this book follow a liturgical organization: part 1, "Advent: O Come, O Come Immanuel"—a time of hopeful waiting for God's promise to be fulfilled; part 2, "Christmas: The Wondrous Gift Is Given"—when God adopts the form of a baby, born in the fullness of time, to demonstrate holy love and humility to humankind; part 3, "Epiphany: To Fill the World with Light"—the manifestation of God in the life of Jesus the Christ that inspires and instructs us all; and part 4, "Praise: Joy to the World"—the all-encompassing, exuberant acknowledgment of this glorious event in human history.

You will notice that most of the readings for the parts on Advent and Christmas are poems. Perhaps writers, ancient and contemporary, found prose too limiting to express the wonder and magnitude that these seasons encompass. Also, more numerous and varied readings are found in the part on Epiphany than in any of the other parts. This festival represents God's continual showing forth of love in the world, and writers abound who can tell of this consequence of the birth of Jesus in prose, poetry, hymns, and stories. Note as well the intimations of pain, suffering, and death in many of these writings. They are selected to show that the Christian faith understands that every aspect of life is transformed in the light of the Incarnation.

With each selection is contextual information about the author or contributor of the work.

May these readings bring you the kind of deep-down, resonating joy that suffuses the soul and nourishes the spirit for the new year to come.

A. Jean Lesher
Editor and Compiler

Part 1

✦ ✦

Advent
O Come, O Come Immanuel

Our time is a time of waiting; waiting is its special destiny.
And every time is a time of waiting, waiting for the breaking in
of eternity. All time runs forward. All time, both history and in
personal life, is expectation. Time itself is waiting, waiting not for
another time, but for that which is eternal.
Paul Tillich (1886–1965)

Introduction

There are two kinds of waiting during the four weeks of Advent before Christmas—one abstract and long-term, the other organic and of shorter duration. The abstract, long-term waiting is for the Messiah, who will redeem the world from suffering and bring peace to humankind. That wait began long before the birth of Jesus and continues now in our desire for world peace, universal love, and the Second Coming of Christ, at the end of time.

The second kind of waiting is from the time of conception to the birth of a baby, the nine-month time that we collapse into the four weeks of the Advent season in the church. During the Advent season we remind ourselves of both the abstract and the organic wait, the hope for a world of peace and the wonder-filled expectation of a birth.

The church calls the moment when the angel talked to Mary about her crucial role in the coming of Jesus the Annunciation, the announcement of a holy event. Her response, also a holy event, is called the Magnificat because of her willingness, her choice—"my soul magnifies the Lord"—to bear Immanuel, God-with-us. For centuries poets and artists have provided insights into these periods of waiting and these events. This part of the book offers some of their responses.

They watch for Christ . . .

After a period of much physical and emotional suffering while on a voyage home to England from Rome, John Henry Newman (1801–1890) composed his most famous hymn, "Lead, Kindly Light." Subsequently he converted from the Church of England to Roman Catholicism and became a priest, the founder of Trinity College in Dublin, and eventually a cardinal. This is a selection from Parochial and Plain Sermons.

THEY watch for Christ:
who are sensitive, eager, apprehensive in mind,
who are awake, alive, quick-sighted,
zealous in honoring him,
who look for him in all that happens, and
who would not be surprised,
who would not be over-agitated or overwhelmed,
if they found that he was coming at once. . . .

This then is to watch:
to be detached from what is present, and
to live in what is unseen;
to live in the thought of Christ as he came once,
and as he will come again;
to desire his second coming,
from our affectionate and grateful
remembrance of his first.

Our time is a time of waiting . . .

Paul Tillich (1886–1965) was forced to leave Germany in 1933 because of his anti-Nazi views. He became a U.S. citizen, and he taught theology at Harvard University and the University of Chicago. This excerpt is from his 1948 book The Shaking of the Foundations.

OUR time is a time of waiting; waiting is its special destiny. And every time is a time of waiting, waiting for the breaking in of eternity. All time runs forward. All time, both history and in personal life, is expectation. Time itself is waiting, waiting not for another time, but for that which is eternal.

Like most other peoples . . .

A liturgist and the publisher for the archdiocese of Chicago, Gabe Huck writes with lyrical passion about the power of the music and the words in worship.

LIKE most other peoples, the Christian people have waited for the solstice. We have waited, and called those waiting days "Advent." We have waited to tell the stories and sing the songs and pray the prayers. We have waited to put into word and melody and procession all that we want to stake our lives on: this place, this earth, this flesh—God's dwelling place.

Before there were theologies for that, there were stories and around the stories there came to be festivity. The stories were not histories or documentaries. They were tales told about a birth by people who had to see everything through the other end of life, the death in which this Jesus triumphed. And so they told of a woman from Galilee called Mary who (as the poet Gerard Manley Hopkins wrote)

> Gave God's infinity
> Dwindled to infancy
> Welcome in womb and breast,
> Birth, milk, and all the rest. . . .

There was this birth. There was the bursting of waters, blood, pushing, cutting cord, fondly wrapping. There was parting at the beginning, as at every beginning. And not only, the stories tell, the blood of birth spilled, but other blood, the world's most innocent blood. It is a true story being told for that, we know, is the way it goes, the way it went, the way it will go: We've all known kings like Herod. It's practically a prerequisite for the job: "Sure, somebody's going to get hurt, a few lives lost, but isn't it worth it?" It comes with the territory.

But then consider how the medieval drama called "The Play of Herod" ends: the escape to Egypt, the hasty retreat of the magi, then the intrusion of the military into the village. The children are murdered and Rachel—the biblical mother—weeps and laments. A comforter is sent by God, but she refuses to be comforted because her children are no more. But this is not the end of the play. Did they somehow invent a happy ending? Nothing of the kind. The ending is not happy, it is a great mystery. For there is a Te Deum sung: "We praise you, God, we confess you as Lord." The greatest chant of praise. This is sung by Mary and Joseph, processing through the audience, but they are joined in their song and procession by the animals and the angels, by the shepherds, by the lamenting Rachel and the parents of Bethlehem, and they are joined by the soldiers and their victims and by Herod. Knowing that (Hopkins again)

> we are wound
> With mercy round and round . . .

they all, incarnate God and all creation, even death, tyrants and martyrs, all process and all sing praise. And we sing too, and find ourselves in the procession.

Today we can't imagine it. We take our Christmas with lots of sugar. And take it in a day. Though we've been baptized into his death, we have little time for or patience with how that death is told at Christmas, a death that confuses lament and praise forever. And no wonder we are careful to keep Christmas at an arm's length. What is Herod in these times? . . .

Not about Bethlehem but about Auschwitz. Or maybe about anyplace the world's Herods (include us in) have wandered. From this year's news: how many places, how many innocent?

Where is that mystery in our Christmastime, the mystery that is victorious cross? It is right there in the stories we tell, the carols we sing, the gifts we give and cards we write, the time we take to process through the dozen days from Christmas to Epiphany, the many ways we have to whisper to one another that the days are numbered now for the world's business-as-usual: somehow, some way we are going to join hands and take the procession all over this earth.

O Antiphons

In the early church in the final days before Christmas, monks would begin to sing the O Antiphons, intoning the Latin words with special solemnity at the vesper hour both before and after they recited Mary's great song of thanksgiving, the Magnificat.

O SAPIENTIA,
QUAE EX ORE ALTISSIMI PRODIISTI,
O Wisdom,
that came forth from the mouth of the Most High,
extending from one end of the universe to the other,
mightily and deftly ordaining all things:
come,
teach us the way of sagacity.

O ADONAI,
ET DUX DOMUS ISRAEL,
O Adonai,
and Prince of the House of Israel,
who appeared to Moses in the flames of a burning bush
and bestowed on him the Law upon Sinai:
come,
ransom us with outstretched arm.

O RADIX JESSE,
QUI STAS IN SIGNUM POPULORUM,
O Stem of Jesse,
who stands forth as a sign unto all peoples,
before whom the kings of the earth shall be silent,
whom the nations shall invoke in prayers:
come,
deliver us, tarry no longer.

O CLAVIS DAVID,
ET SCEPTRUM DOMUS ISRAEL,
O Key of David,
and Scepter of the House of Israel,
who opens, and no man closes;
who shuts and no man opens:
come,
bring forth from the house of captivity the vanquished,
who sit in darkness and the shadow of death.

O ORIENS,
SPLENDOR LUCIS AETERNAE,
ET SOL JUSTITIAE,
O Day-Spring,
Splendor of Eternal Light,
and Sun of Justice:
come,
enlighten those who sit in darkness
and in the shadow of death.

O EMMANUEL,
REX ET LEGIFER NOSTER,
O Emmanuel,
King and our Lawgiver,
the Desire of all nations and their Savior:
come,
save us, Lord, our God.

In the beginning was the Word . . .

The most powerful statement in the Bible about the mystery of the Incarnation is found in these few words from John 1:1–5,14–16.

I N the beginning was the Word,
    and the Word was with God,
    and the Word was God.
He was in the beginning with God.
All things came into being through him,
    and without him not one thing
    came into being.
What has come into being in him was life,
    and the life was the light of all people.
    The light shines in the darkness,
    and the darkness did not overcome it.

And the Word became flesh
    and lived among us,
    and we have seen his glory,
    the glory as of a father's only son,
    full of grace and truth. . . .

From his fullness we have all received,
    grace upon grace.

In the beginning . . .

A poet, musician, and liturgist, Miriam Therese Winter is professor of liturgy, worship, and spirituality at Hartford Seminary in Connecticut and a Medical Mission Sister. She has written several books on liturgy, including Woman-Prayer, WomanSong: Resources for Ritual, *from which this selection based on Genesis 1, John 1:1–14, and Proverbs 8:22–31 is taken.*

IN the beginning
before the mountains had been shaped,
before the hills,
before the beginning of the earth:
In the beginning,
before the birdsong
or the breath of life
lifted its gift
to the warmth of the sun:
In the beginning
was the Word
and the Word was with God
when God established the heavens,
when God drew a circle on the face of the deep,
when God marked out the foundations of the earth,
the Word was with God,
and the Word was God.
The Word was Power,
empowering all,
and the Word was Light,
enlightening all,
and the Word was Love,
loving all.
And the Word became flesh
and lived with us;
Ultimate Truth,
Source of Grace,
made of our world
a holy place,
as it was in the beginning
is now,
and shall be
always and forever.

With a Measure of Light

Arthur Edward Waite (1857–1942) was Brooklyn-born but immigrated to England early in his life. He was an editor, an author, a poet, and a leading scholar of mysticism. This selection is from a devotional book entitled Five Minutes a Day.

WITH a measure of light and a measure of shade,
The world of old by the Word was made;
By the shade and light was the Word concealed,
And the Word in flesh to the world revealed
Is by outward sense and its forms obscured:
The spirit within is the long lost Word,
Besought by the world of the soul in pain
Through a world of words which are void and vain.
O never while shadow and light are blended
Shall the world's Word-quest or its woe be ended,
And never the world of its wounds made whole
Till the Word made flesh be the Word made soul.

The people who walked in darkness . . .

The most beloved of prophecies for the coming of Christ is in this passage from the Old Testament book of the prophet Isaiah, chapter 9, verses 2–7. It speaks to every age.

THE people who walked in darkness
have seen a great light;
    those who lived in a land of deep darkness—
    on them light has shined. . . .
For the yoke of their burden,
    and the bar across their shoulders,
    the rod of their oppressor,
    you have broken as on the day of Midian.
For all the boots of the tramping warriors
    and all the garments rolled in blood
    shall be burned as fuel for the fire.

For a child has been born for us,
    a son given to us;
    authority rests upon his shoulders;
    and he is named
    Wonderful Counselor, Mighty God,
    Everlasting Father, Prince of Peace.
    His authority shall grow continually,
    and there shall be endless peace
    for the throne of David and his kingdom.
    He will establish and uphold it
    with justice and with righteousness
    from his time onward and forevermore.
    The zeal of the LORD of hosts will do this.

The Visit

Medical Mission Sister Miriam Therese Winter has spent time as a relief worker in Cambodia and Ethiopia while filling her role as professor of liturgy and spirituality at Hartford Seminary.

READER: The angel said to Mary:
               "The Holy Spirit will come upon you,
               and the power of the Most High
               will overshadow you,
               and the child to be born of you
               will be called the Child of God." (Lk 1:35)

Leader: May the One who comes,
               come again in us.

All: May the One who comes
               become in us
               love-made-visible to all. Amen.

Voice One: She was visited by an angel,
               with the name of a man,
               and was asked to do something
               no one on earth
               had ever done before.

All: Hail, Mary!
               Woman among women,
               heroine of all the earth.

Voice One: She was filled with the Holy Spirit:
               bone of her bone,
               flesh of her flesh,
               blood of her blood,
               God with us,
               God among us
               in a very womanly way.

All: Hail, Mary!
               Woman among women,
               heroine of all the earth.

Voice One: Transformation,
Transubstantiation,
woman's whole being,
body and blood,
soul and spirit,
is living Eucharist!
Give thanks to God,
and praise,
all women,
all our days.

All: Hail, Mary!
Woman among women,
heroine of all the earth.

Voice One: God always favors
the favorless,
those cast aside,
a burden to society
or of little consequence.
A woman,
least among least,
chosen by God
to make God present:
our first New Testament priest.

All: Hail, Mary!
Woman among women,
heroine of all the earth.

Annunciation

Denise Levertov is the daughter of a Welsh woman and of a Russian Jewish man who converted to Christianity and became an Anglican priest in England, where Denise was born and raised. In 1955 she became a U.S. citizen. A poet, essayist, editor, translator, educator, and antiwar protester, she reflects her social concerns through much of her writing.

WE know the scene: the room, variously furnished,
    almost always a lectern, a book: always
the tall lily.

         Arrived on solemn grandeur of great wings,
the angelic ambassador, standing or hovering,
whom she acknowledges, a guest.

But we are told of meek obedience. No one mentions
courage.
            The engendering Spirit
did not enter her without consent.
            God waited.

She was free
to accept or to refuse, choice
integral to humanness.

Aren't there annunciations
of one sort or another
in most lives?

            Some unwillingly
undertake great destinies,
enact them in sullen pride,
uncomprehending.

            More often
those moments
    when roads of light and storm
    open from darkness in a man or woman
are turned away from
in dread, in a wave of weakness, in despair
and with relief.
Ordinary lives continue.

God does not smithe them.
But the gates close, the pathway vanishes.

She had been a child who played, ate, slept
like any other child—but unlike others,
wept only for pity, laughed
in joy not triumph,
compassion and intelligence
fused in her, indivisible.
Called to a destiny more momentous
than any in all of Time,
she did not quail,
              only asked
a simple, "How can this be?"
and gravely, courteously,
took to heart the angel's reply,
perceiving instantly
the astounding ministry she was offered:

to bear in her womb
Infinite weight and lightness: to carry
in hidden, finite inwardness,
nine months of Eternity; to contain
in slender vase of being
the sum of power—
in narrow flesh,
the sum of light.

              Then bring to birth,
push out into air, a Man-child
needing like any other,
milk and love—
but who was God.

This was the minute no one speaks of,
when she could still refuse.

A breath unbreathed,
              Spirit,
                   suspended,
waiting.

She did not cry, "I cannot, I am not worthy."
nor, "I have not the strength."
She did not submit with gritted teeth,
                    raging, coerced.
Bravest of all humans,
                    consent illumined her.
The room filled with its light,
the lily glowed in it,
                    and the iridescent wings.
Consent,
                    courage unparalleled,
opened her utterly.

Annunciation

John Donne (1572–1631) converted from Roman Catholicism to the Church of England. He took holy orders in 1615, and became best known for his eloquent preaching. Most of his poems and prose works were published after his death. Donne is considered a great seventeenth-century English metaphysical poet and rhetorician. This selection is from La Corona, a sequence of seven sonnets intended to be an endless wreath of praise, similar to traditional meditations on the Virgin Mary.

S ALVATION *to all that will is nigh;*
That All, which always is All everywhere,
Which cannot sin, and yet all sins must bear,
Which cannot die, yet cannot choose but die,
Lo, faithful Virgin, yields himself to lie
In prison, in thy womb; and though he there
Can take no sin, nor thou give, ye he will wear
Taken from thence, flesh, which death's force may try.
Ere by the spheres time was created, thou
Wast in his mind, who is thy Son, and Brother;
Whom thou conceiv'st, conceiv'd; yeah thou art now
Thy Maker's maker, and thy Father's mother;
Thou hast light in dark; and shutst in little room,
Immensity cloistered in thy dear womb.

Annunciation to Mary

Rainer Maria Rilke (1875–1926) is generally considered the greatest German lyric poet since Goethe. Born in Prague, he lived twelve years in Paris and in Germany, and he spent time in Russia.

NOT that an angel came in, understand,
was she alarmed. As little as others start
when a sunray or beam of moonlight darts
into a room and busies itself here and there,
would she have been made angry by the guise
in which an angel came. Could she surmise
how tedious angels find such tarrying here?
(Oh, if we knew how pure she was! A hind,
once when resting, saw her in the wood,
and gazing lost itself until it could—
all without any coupling with its kind—
conceive the unicorn, pure animal,
the beast of light.) Not that he entered, but
that he bowed down so close to her the face
of a young man, this angel, that her gaze
as she glanced up joined with his, as if all
outside there suddenly seemed void and what
the millions saw, were doing, suffering,
seemed forced into them: only she and he—
the seeing and seen, the eye and eye's delight
nowhere else but in this one place. See!
this is frightening. And they were both afraid.
Then the angel sang his melody.

nnunciation

Reynolds Price is professor of English at Duke University, a novelist, a drama-
tist, and a recipient of many poetry awards. This selection is from his book Nine
Mysteries.

THE angel Gabriel was sent from God to a city in Galilee named
Nazareth to a virgin promised to a man named Joseph of the
house of David. The virgin's name was Mary. Coming in on her he
said "Rejoice, beloved! The Lord is with you."

Luke 1:26–28

Annunciation

The angel tries to imagine *need*.
Till now he has not stood near a girl—
Odd generals, magistrates, prophets in skins—
And since his mission is to cry "Beloved!"
And warn of the coming down on her
Of absolute need, he pauses to study
Her opaque hands—both open toward him—
And strains to know what need could draw
The Heart of Light to settle on this
Dun child, clay-brown, when curved space
Burns with willing vessels compounded of air.
He feels he is failing; is balked by skin,
Hair, eyes dense as coal.
"Beloved" clogs his throat. He blinks.
Nothing needs this. He has misunderstood.

The girl though has passed through shock to honor
And begins to smile. She plans to speak.
Her dry lips part. *"Me."* She nods.

The low room fills that instant with dark
Which is also wind—a room not two
Of her short steps wide, plugged with dark
(Outside it is three, March afternoon).
In the cube, black as a cold star's core,
One small point shines—her lean face
Licked by a joy no seraph has shown,
An ardor of need held back for this
And bound to kill.

But slowly she dims,
The room recovers, she opens a fist.

The angel can speak. "Rejoice, beloved!"

The girl laughs one high note, polite—
Cold news—then kneels by her cot to thank him.

Magnificat

After the Annunciation, Mary went to visit her kinswoman Elizabeth, who was expecting the birth of John the Baptist. Elizabeth's baby "leaped in her womb" when Mary walked in. Elizabeth told her in great joy: "'Blessed are you among women, and blessed is the fruit of your womb.'" Mary responded with the beautiful words of the Magnificat (Luke 1:46–55).

AND Mary said,
"My soul magnifies the Lord,
and my spirit rejoices in God my Savior,
for he has looked with favor on the lowliness of his servant.
Surely, from now on all generations will call me blessed;
for the Mighty One has done great things for me,
    and holy is his name.
His mercy is for those who fear him
    from generation to generation.
He has shown strength with his arm;
    he has scattered the proud in the thoughts of their hearts.
He has brought down the powerful from their thrones,
    and lifted up the lowly;
he has filled the hungry with good things,
    and sent the rich away empty.
He has helped his servant Israel,
    in remembrance of his mercy,
according to the promise he made to our ancestors,
    to Abraham and to his descendants forever."

Magnificat

This poem comes from an anonymous Chilean woman and is found in a collection entitled Soul Weavings, *edited by Lyn Klug.*

WITH pride and dignity I sing my song of joy
    when I feel the Lord's presence;
I am poor and very ordinary,
    but one day the Lord looked upon me
And the history of the poor will give witness to my joy.
God is unfettered and unpredictable,
    He is called our great friend
And throughout our history He has favored those of us
    who are weak.
His triumphant force shows itself each day
    when He exposes the foolishness of the powerful.
He uncovers the feet of clay of those in power,
    and nourishes the yearning of the poor.
To those who come hungry He gives bread and wine.
And to the wealthy He exposes their selfishness
    and the emptiness of their ways.
This is God's desire: always to favor the poor.
Now finally we can walk.
He is faithful to His promises.

Joseph's Suspicion

This selection is from a book by Rainer Maria Rilke (1875–1926) entitled The Life of the Virgin Mary. *The Bible verses concerning this episode are from* Matthew 1:19–24.

AND the angel, taking due pains, told
the man who clenched his fists:
But can't you see in her robe's every fold
that she is cool as the Lord's morning mists?

But the other, gazing gloomily, just murmured:
What is it has wrought this change in her?
Then cried the angel to him: Carpenter,
can't you see yet that God is acting here?

Because you plane the planks, in your pride would
you really make the Lord God answerable
who unpretentiously from the same wood
makes the leaves burst forth, the young buds swell?

He understood that. And now as he raised
his frightened glance toward the angel who
was gone already . . . slowly the man drew
his heavy cap off. Then in song he praised.

Joseph Was an Old Man

This traditional carol was popular in medieval England and ran on for dozens of verses, depending on the religious season.

JOSEPH was an old man,
    And an old man was he,
When he wedded Mary
    In the land of Galilee.

Joseph and Mary walked
    Through an orchard good,
Where was cherries and berries
    So red as any blood.

Joseph and Mary walked
    Through an orchard green,
Where was berries and cherries
    As thick as might be seen.

O then bespoke Mary,
    With words so meek and mild,
"Pluck me one cherry, Joseph,
    For I am with child."

O then bespoke Joseph,
    With answer most unkind,
"Let him pluck thee a cherry
    That brought thee now with child."

O then bespoke the baby
    Within his mother's womb—
"Bow down then the tallest tree
    For my mother to have some."

Then bowed down the highest tree
    Unto his mother's hand.
Then she cried, "See, Joseph,
    I have cherries at command."

O then bespake Joseph—
    "I have done Mary wrong;
But now cheer up, my dearest,
    And do not be cast down.

"O eat your cherries, Mary,
    O eat your cherries now,
O eat your cherries, Mary,
    That grow upon the bough."

Then Mary plucked a cherry,
    As red as any blood;
Then Mary she went homewards
    All with her heavy load.

The Mother of God

*William Butler Yeats (1865–1939) was born in Dublin, Ireland, of Protestant
parents. He founded the Abbey Theatre and became the leader of the Irish literary revival. By the age of forty-three, he had published one hundred volumes of
poems, plays, and prose works.*

THE threefold terror of love; a fallen flare
    Through the hollow of an ear;
Wings beating about the room;
The terror of all terrors that I bore
The Heavens in my womb.
Had I not found content among the shows
Every common woman knows,
Chimney corner, garden walk,
Or rocky cistern where we tread the clothes
And gather all the talk?
What is this flesh I purchased with my pains,
This fallen star my milk sustains,
This love that makes my heart's blood stop
Or strikes a sudden chill into my bones
And bids my hair stand up?

A Message Came to a Maiden Young

This traditional Dutch nineteenth-century verse comes from Nederlandsch Volksliederenboek.

A MESSAGE came to a maiden young;
    The angel stood beside her,
In shining robes and with golden tongue,
    He told what should betide her:
        The maid was lost in wonder—
        Her world was rent asunder—
           Ah! how could she
           Christ's mother be
        By God's most high decree!

No greater news could a messenger bring;
    For 'twas from that young mother
He came, who walked on the earth as a king,
    And yet was all men's brother:
        His truth has spread like leaven,
        'Twill marry earth to heaven,
           Till all agree
           In charity
        To dwell from sea to sea.

He came, God's Word to the world here below;
    And round him there did gather
A band who found that this Teacher to know
    Was e'en to know the Father:
        He healed the sick who sought him,
        Forgave the foes who fought him;
           Beside the Sea
           Of Galilee
        He set the nations free.

And sometimes trumpets from Sion ring out,
    And tramping comes, and drumming—
"Thy Kingdom come," so we cry; and they shout,
    "It comes!" and still 'tis coming—
        Far, far ahead, to win us,
        Yet with us, nay within us;
           Till all shall see
           That King is he,
           The Love from Galilee!

Mater Dei

Irish poet and writer Padraic Fallon (1905–1974) was a customs official for over forty years. Even some of his radio plays are written in verse.

IN March the seed
Fell, when the month leaned over, looking
Down into her valley.
And none but the woman knew it where she sat
In the tree of her veins and tended him

The red and ripening Adam of the year.
Her autumn was late and human.
Trees were nude, the lights were on the pole
All night when he came,
Her own man;
In the cry of a child she sat, not knowing
That this was a stranger.

Milk ran wild
Across the heavens. Imperiously He
Sipped at the delicate beakers she proffered him.
How was she to know
How huge a body she was, how she corrected
The very tilt of the earth on its new course?

Den dat little man . . .

After her own narrow escape from slavery, Sojourner Truth (ca. 1797–1883) gave her time to supporting the causes of black people's and women's rights. Suffragist Frances Gage described her electrifying speech at a women's rights meeting in 1851 in the article "Sojourner Truth Speaks in Meeting," from which this excerpt is taken.

Den dat little man in black dar, he say women can't have as much rights as men, 'cause Christ wan't a woman! Whar did your Christ come from?" Rolling thunder couldn't have stilled that crowd, as did those deep, wonderful tones, as she stood there with outstretched arms and eyes of fire. Raising her voice still louder, she repeated, "Whar did your Christ come from? From God and a woman! Man had nothin' to do wid Him." Oh, what a rebuke that was to that little man!

Part 2

➤ ◄

Christmas
The Wondrous Gift Is Given

The earth has grown old with its burden of care,
But at Christmas it always is young.
The heart of the jewel burns lustrous and fair,
And its soul full of music bursts forth on the air,
When the song of the angels is sung.
Phillips Brooks (1835–1893)

Introduction

The story of Christmas is so down-to-earth, so concrete in its images, and so memorable for all ages who can relate to things such as pregnancy, rejection, miserable surroundings, farm animals, cold hillsides, fear, wonder, and joy.

In just a few phrases, the Bible relates the events of the Christmas story so matter-of-factly that the story leaves abundant room for artists and poets to imagine what happened. What was in the minds of the innkeepers who would not give Mary and Joseph a room for a birthing? What kind of experiences did the shepherds have on their hillside and in the stable? Why on earth did God pick such a smelly, dirty place for Jesus to be born?

We all have our own thoughts and images about what happened whenever and wherever it did. We can also feel wonder and gratitude that it did happen.

Bethlehem

A professor and poet, Bliss Carman (1861–1929) lived most of his life in New Canaan, Connecticut. This poem is based on an old French carol. It first appeared in the early part of the twentieth century in a magazine entitled Pictorial Review.

L ONG was the road to Bethlehem,
Where Joseph and his Mary came.
They are travel-worn, the day grows late,
As they reach the town with its towered gate—
The city of David's royal line—
And the stars of eve are beginning to shine.
They must seek a place where the poor may rest,
For Mary is weary and overpressed.

AND IT IS THE SIXTH HOUR.

They come to an inn and knock on the door,
Asking a little space,—no more
Than a humble shelter in their need.
The innkeeper gives them scanty heed.
Little for strangers does he care—
His house is full. They must seek elsewhere.
Fearing to find no place that day,
Heavy at heart they turn away.

AND IT IS THE SEVENTH HOUR.

In weariness and sore perplexed,
To a larger house they venture next.
Joseph for pity's sake begs again
A lodging for Mary in her pain.
They are poor Galileans, plain to be told—
Their garments are worn, their sandals are old.
The fat innkeeper jingles his keys,
And refuses shelter to such as these.

AND IT IS THE NINTH HOUR.

Where now they turn the woman is kind,
The place is crowded, still she would find
Room for them somehow—moved at the sight
Of this gentle girl in her urgent plight,

Who tells of her hope and her strength far spent,
And seems to her woman's heart God-sent,
But the surly landlord roars in wrath
And sends them forth on their lonely path.

AND IT IS THE ELEVENTH HOUR.

Still seeking a place to lay them down,
They come at length, on the edge of the town,
To a cattle-shed with sagging door,
Thankful for only the stable floor,
When an old gray donkey crowds to the wall
To make them room in his straw-laid stall.
And the cattle low at the stifled wail
Of a woman's voice in sore travail.

IT IS MIDNIGHT AND MARY'S HOUR.

Over the place a great new star
Sheds wonder and glory beheld afar,
While all through the height of heaven there flies
The word of a seraph voice that cries,
"Glory to God, this wondrous morn
On earth the Saviour Christ is born."

Christmas Carol

Phillips Brooks (1835–1893) was born in Boston, graduated from Harvard University, and became best known at home and abroad for the inspiring sermons he preached during his twenty-two-year ministry at Trinity Church in his hometown. Thousands came to hear this unpretentious man, who presented the faith in an appealing combination of power, serenity, and charm.

THE earth has grown old with its burden of care,
But at Christmas it always is young.
The heart of the jewel burns lustrous and fair,
And its soul full of music bursts forth on the air,
When the song of the angels is sung.

It is coming, Old Earth, it is coming to-night!
On the snowflakes that cover thy sod.
The feet of the Christ-child fall gentle and white,
And the voice of the Christ-child tells out with delight
That we are the Children of God.

On the sad and the lonely, the wretched and poor,
The voice of the Christ-child shall fall;
And to every blind wanderer open the door
Of hope that he dared not to dream of before,
With a sunshine and welcome for all.

The feet of the humblest may walk in the field
Where the feet of the Holiest trod,
This, then, is the marvel to mortals revealed
When the silvery trumpets of Christmas have pealed,
That we are the children of God.

The Oxen

English novelist and poet Thomas Hardy (1840–1928) studied to be an architect before moving to London and writing poems about rural life. His first novel, Far from the Madding Crowd, published in 1874, was a success, and others followed. This poem was inspired by a legend.

CHRISTMAS Eve, and twelve of the clock.
"Now they are all on their knees,"
An elder said as we sat in a flock
By the embers in hearthside ease.

We pictured the meek mild creature where
They dwelt in the strawy pen,
Nor did it occur to one of us there
To doubt they were kneeling then.

So fair a fancy few would weave
In these years! Yet, I feel,
If someone said on Christmas Eve,
"Come; see the oxen kneel,

"In the lonely barton by yonder coomb
Our childhood used to know,"
I should go with him in the gloom,
Hoping it might be so.

Some say . . .

Marcellus, an officer of the king of Denmark, speaks the following lines in act 1, scene 1, of Hamlet, the great tragedy by William Shakespeare (1564–1616). He and his fellows are musing about the winter's night in front of the castle in Elsinore.

SOME say that ever 'gainst that season comes
Wherein our Saviour's birth is celebrated,
The bird of dawning singeth all night long;
And then, they say, no spirit can walk abroad;
The nights are wholesome; then no planets strike,
No fairy takes, nor witch hath power to charm,
So hallow'd and so gracious is the time.

Carol 3

A most important and prolific Latin American baroque writer, Sor Juana Inés de la Cruz (1651–1695) was born in colonial Mexico when women could not pursue education except in the church. She became a nun and wrote essays, plays, love sonnets, and poems. Her carol sequences—"Carol 3" is excerpted here—were created for large groups of people of different classes and races to enjoy in cathedrals.

1. Where are you going, children?
   2. To Bethlehem,
      to see wonders,
      that are to be seen.
1. Tell us, children,
      how do you know this?
2. In the air it is sung by Angels
      with loud voices. Listen, heed!

Verses

Today you see in a stable
the Word speechless,
Greatness in smallness,
Immensity in blankets.

All. Such wonders!

From a Star the Sun is born,
the Ocean reaches a shore,
and a Flower blooms,
infant Fruit awakens.

All. Such wonders!

The Immutable is in pain,
the burning Fire cools down,
Divinity becomes human,
and Rectitude inclines.

All. Such wonders!

The One before all tremble, trembles;
Sovereignty steps down,
Courage diminishes
and Laughter itself cries.

All. Such wonders!

The earth is Heaven now
in this Night that is Dawn;
Eternity is temporary,
and death is what Life was.

All. Such wonders!

Truth is today disguised,
Strength weakens,
Omnipotence shrinks
and clear Light is now eclipsed.

All. Such wonders!

Now Royalty is humble,
now Happiness is tears,
now hardships are tenderness
and Justice is now Mercy.

All. Such wonders!

Now Wealth is poverty,
and the Powerful a beggar,
and the Lion, always victor,
is now Lamb for sacrifice.

All. Such wonders!

He who had no beginning,
his being of Time begins;
the Creator, as a creature,
is now subject to our griefs.

All. Such wonders!

Men: Hear these wonders
that are more than human joys:
God is Man, Man is God,
and among them they are in touch.

All. Such wonders!

Here It Begins

This reading by Michael Norton was found in a Christmas letter from a Minnesota church office. The church office thought its origin was a hymn sung by a college choir at a Christmas concert.

HERE it begins, in the dark before dawning.
Here, in a barn full of animal smells.
The warm breath of cattle, the sounds of the morning,
Here without tinsel or tolling of bells.

This is the Word Who was there at the Making?
This is the pure and unbearable Light?
Tiny and wrinkle-faced, squalling and shaking
Small fists at the vast and implacable night?

Who can believe this impossible fable?
And He is stronger than all of our sins.
A light in the darkness, a child in the stable.
Stronger than death itself, here it begins.

What Child Is This

Although manager of an English marine insurance company, William Chatterton Dix (1837–1898) was also a writer of fine hymns. The tune for this selection is from a beloved English folk tune, "Greensleeves," which first appeared in England in 1580.

WHAT child is this, who, laid to rest,
On Mary's lap is sleeping?
Whom angels greet with anthems sweet
While shepherds watch are keeping?
This, this is Christ the king,
Whom shepherds guard and angels sing;
Haste, haste to bring him laud,
The babe, the son of Mary!

Why lies he in such mean estate
Where ox and ass are feeding?
Good Christian, fear; for sinners here
The silent Word is pleading.
Nails, spear shall pierce him through,
The cross be borne for me, for you;
Hail, hail the Word made flesh,
The babe, the son of Mary!

So bring him incense, gold, and myrrh;
Come, peasant, king, to own him;
The King of kings salvation brings;
Let loving hearts enthrone him.
Raise, raise the song on high,
The Virgin sings her lullaby;
Joy, joy, for Christ is born,
The babe, the son of Mary!

In Preparation for the Nativity

This prayer from the Great Church of Constantinople grew out of the liturgical rites of the Byzantine Empire, 395–1453 C.E. Many of the rites continue to be used in Orthodox churches throughout the world today.

TODAY the virgin is on her way to the cave where she will give birth in a manner beyond understanding to the Word who is in all eternity. Rejoice, therefore, universe, when you hear it heralded: with the angels and the shepherds, glorify him who chose to be seen as a new-born babe, while remaining God in all eternity.

From "At the Manger"

Wystan Hugh Auden (1907–1973), born in York, England, and educated at Oxford, joined the Republican forces in Spain in the mid–1930s. His early writings reflected his political views. After converting to Anglicanism in the early 1940s, he wrote more on religious themes. This selection is from "At the Manger," part 1 of his play-poem For the Time Being: A Christmas Oratorio.

MARY:
O shut your bright eyes that mine must endanger
With their watchfulness; protected by its shade
Escape from my care: what can you discover
From my tender look but how to be afraid?
Love can but confirm the more it would deny.
    Close your bright eye.

Sleep. What have you learned from the womb that bore you
But an anxiety your Father cannot feel?
Sleep. What will the flesh that I gave do for you,
Or my mother love, but tempt you from His will?
Why was I chosen to teach His Son to weep?
    Little One, sleep

Dream. In human dreams earth ascends to Heaven
Where no one need pray nor ever feel alone.
In your first few hours of life here, O have you
Chosen already what death must be your own?
How soon will you start on the Sorrowful Way?
    Dream while you may.

Every Man Heart Lay Down

Lorenz Graham (1902–1989) was born in the parsonage of Saint James A. M. E. Church in New Orleans, the son of an African Methodist Episcopal minister. A missionary uncle took Graham to Africa with him in 1924 to work in Liberia and Sierra Leone in educational programs. Graham studied the West African idiom, and using it, wrote a collection of Bible stories published in 1946 as How God Fix Jonah. This "spoken song," as he called it, comes from that collection.

LONG time past
Before you papa live
Before him papa live
Before him pa's papa live—

Long time past
Before them big tree live
Before them big tree's papa live—
That time God live.

And God look on the world
What He done make
And Him heart no lay down.
And He walk about in the town
To see the people
And He sit down in the palaver house
To know the people
And He vex too much.
And God say
      "Nev mind.
      The people no hear My Word
      The people no walk My way
      Nev mind.
      I going break the world and lose the people
      I going make the day dark
      And the night I going make hot.
      I going make water that side where land belong
      And land that side where water belong.
      And I going make a new country
      And make a new people."

Now this time
God's one small boy—Him small pican—hear God's Word
And the pican grieve for people
So he go fore God's face
And make talk for him Pa.
>"Pa, I come for beg You," so he say
>"I come for beg You,
>Don't break the world
>What You done make.
>Don't lose the people
>What You done care for.
>I beg You
>Make it I go
>I talk to people
>I walk with people
>Bye-m-bye they savvy the way."

And the pican go down softly softly
And hold God's foot.
So God look on Him small boy
And Him heart be soft again
And God say
>"Aye My son,
>When you beg me so
>I no can vex.
>Left me now, but hear me good:
>If you go you must be born like a man
>And you must live like a man
>And you must have hurt and have hunger.
>And hear me good:
>Men will hate you
>And they will flog you
>And bye-m-bye they will kill you
>And I no going put My hand there."

And the pican say
>"I agree!"

And bye-m-bye God call Mary
To be Ma for the pican
Now Mary be new wife for Joseph
And Joseph ain't touch Mary self
So first time Joseph vex.
But God say
    "Nev mind, Joseph,
    This be God palaver."
    And Joseph heart lay down.

And God see one king who try for do good
For all him people
And God say
    "Ahah, Now I send My son
    For be new king."
    And God send star to call the king.

And in a far country
God hear a wise man call Him name
And God say to the wise man
    "I send My son to be new wise man,
    Go now with the star."
And the star call
And the wise man follow.

And by the waterside
Men lay down for take rest
And they hear fine music in the sky
Like all the stars make song,
And they fear.
And all the dark make bright like day
And the water shine like fire
And no man can savvy
And they hearts turn over.
But God's angel come
And God's angel say
    "Make glad, all people,
    God's pican be born in Bethlehem."
And the people say "Oh."

And the wise man and the king
And the country people come to Bethlehem
And the star come low and stop.
But when they go for mansion house
The star no be there.
And when they go for Big Man's house
The star no be there.
And bye-m-bye when they go for hotel
The star no be there gain—
But the wise man say
  "Ahah, the star be by the small house
  Where cattle sleep!"
And it was so.

And they find Joseph and Mary
And the small small pican
Fold up in country cloth
And the king bring gold for gift
And the wise man bring fine oil
And the country people bring new rice.

And they look on the God pican
And every man heart lay down.

Nativity

James Montgomery (1771–1854), an English journalist and editor, wrote and spoke out frequently in his newspaper the Sheffield Iris *against social injustice. His parents were Moravian missionaries. This beloved hymn, one of four hundred that he wrote, was first printed in his paper on Christmas Eve 1816.*

ANGELS, from the realms of glory,
Wing your flight o'er all the earth;
Ye who sang creation's story,
Now proclaim Messiah's birth:
Come and worship,
Worship Christ the new-born King.

Shepherds in the field abiding,
Watching o'er your flocks by night,
God with man is now residing;
Yonder shines the infant-light:
Come and worship,
Worship Christ the new-born King.

Sages, leave your contemplations;
Brighter visions beam afar;
Seek the great Desire of nations;
Ye have seen His natal star:
Come and worship,
Worship Christ the new-born King.

Saints before the altar bending,
Watching long in hope and fear,
Suddenly the Lord, descending,
In his temple shall appear:
Come and worship,
Worship Christ the new-born King.

Sinners, wrung with true repentance,
Doom'd for guilt to endless pains,
Justice now revokes the sentence,
Mercy calls you—break your chains:
Come and worship,
Worship Christ the new-born King.

Nativity

In John Donne's (1572–1631) writing, one finds passionate feeling and intellect combined, so that his work might be equally well described as illustrative of passionate intellect or intellectual passion. Considered a fine metaphysical writer in both poetry and prose, Donne also was a great preacher. This selection is from La Corona, a sequence of sonnets intended in praise of the Virgin Mary.

IMMENSITY *cloistered in thy dear womb,*
Now leaves his well-beloved imprisonment,
There he hath made himself to his intent
Weak enough, now into our world to come;
But Oh, for thee, for him, hath the Inn no room?
Yet lay him in this stall, and from the Orient,
Stars, and wisemen will travel to prevent
The effect of Herod's jealous general doom.
Seest thou, my Soul, with thy faith's eyes, how he
Which fills all place, yet none holds him, doth lie?
Was not his pity towards thee wondrous high,
That would have need to be pitied by thee?
Kiss him, and with him into Egypt go,
With his kind mother, who partakes thy woe.

A Christmas Carol

Christina Rossetti (1830–1894) was a prolific and popular poet in nineteenth-century England, although many of her poems are considered gloomy today. She was born in London of Italian-English parents, and her family was devout Anglo-Catholic.

BEFORE the paling of the stars,
Before the winter morn,
Before the earliest cock-crow
   Jesus Christ was born:
   Born in a stable,
   Cradled in a manger,
In the world His hands had made
   Born a stranger.

Priest and king lay fast asleep
   In Jerusalem,
Young and old lay fast asleep
   In crowded Bethlehem:
Saint and angel, ox and ass,
   Kept a watch together,
Before the Christmas daybreak
   In the winter weather.

Jesus on His mother's breast
   In the stable cold,
Spotless Lamb of God was He,
   Shepherd of the fold:
Let us kneel with Mary maid,
   With Joseph bent and hoary,
With saint and angel, ox and ass,
   To hail the King of Glory.

'Twas in the Moon of Wintertime

Father Jean de Brébeuf was a Jesuit missionary among the Huron people in Canada in the early seventeenth century. Early in the twentieth century, Jesse Middleton translated this poem by de Brébeuf from its original French into English and added some Huron folk symbols, such as rabbit skin for swaddling clothes.

'TWAS in the moon of wintertime, when all the birds had fled,
    that mighty Gitchi Manitou sent angel choirs instead;
Before their lights the stars grew dim, and wondering hunters heard
    the hymn:
    Jesus Emmanuel, Jesus is born, in *excelsis gloria.*

Within a lodge of broken bark the tender babe was found;
    a ragged robe of rabbit skin enwrapped his beauty round;
But as the hunter braves drew nigh, the angel song rang loud and
    high:
    Jesus Emmanuel, Jesus is born, in *excelsis gloria.*

The earliest moon of wintertime is not so round and fair
    as was the ring of glory on the helpless infant there.
The chiefs from far before him knelt with gifts of fox and
    beaver pelt.
    Jesus Emmanuel, Jesus is born, in *excelsis gloria.*

O children of the forest free, O seed of Manitou,
    the holy Child of earth and heaven is born today for you.
Come kneel before the radiant Child, who brings you beauty, peace,
    so mild.
    Jesus Emmanuel, Jesus is born, in *excelsis gloria.*

Sharon's Prayer

Chicago native John Shea is a theologian, writer, and storyteller who has inspired, instructed, and delighted audiences all over the world.

SHE was five,
sure of the facts,
and recited them
with slow solemnity,
convinced every word
was revelation.
She said

they were so poor
they had only peanut butter and jelly
sandwiches to eat
and they went a long way from home
without getting lost. The lady rode
a donkey, the man walked, and the baby
was inside the lady.
They had to stay in a stable
with an ox and an ass but the
Three Rich Men found them
because a star lited the roof.
Shepherds came and you could
pet the sheep but not feed them.
Then the baby was borned.
And do you know who he was?

Her quarter eyes inflated
to silver dollars.

The baby was God!

And she jumped in the air,
whirled round, dove into the sofa,
and buried her head
under the cushion
which is the only proper response
to the Good News
of the Incarnation.

O Little Town of Bethlehem

A big man with an innate gentleness and cheerfulness, the Right Reverend Phillips Brooks (1835–1893) won an international reputation for his sermons during his long ministry at Trinity Church in Boston. He wrote this beloved Christmas carol in 1868 for Sunday school children.

O LITTLE town of Bethlehem,
How still we see thee lie!
Above thy deep and dreamless sleep
　　The silent stars go by;
Yet in thy dark streets shineth
　　The everlasting light;
The hopes and fears of all the years
　　Are met in thee to-night.

O morning stars, together
　　Proclaim the holy birth,
And praises sing to God the king,
　　And peace to [all the] earth;
For Christ is born of Mary;
　　And, gathered all above,
While mortals sleep, the angels keep
　　Their watch of wond'ring love.

How silently, how silently,
　　The wondrous gift is given!
So God imparts to human hearts
　　The blessings of his heaven.
No ear may hear his coming;
　　But in this world of sin,
Where meek souls will receive him, still
　　The dear Christ enters in.

Where children pure and happy
　　Pray to the blessèd Child,
Where misery cries out to thee,
　　Son of the mother mild;
Where charity stands watching
　　And faith holds wide the door,
The dark night wakes, the glory breaks,
　　And Christmas comes once more.

O holy Child of Bethlehem,
    Descend to us, we pray;
Cast out our sin, and enter in,
    Be born in us to-day.
We hear the Christmas Angels
    The great glad tidings tell:
O come to us, abide with us,
    Our Lord Immanuel.

The Christ-Child Lay on Mary's Lap

Gilbert Keith Chesterton (1874–1936) was beloved in England for his exuberant personality and rotund figure as well as for his fine poems, essays, novels, and short stories. The three major subjects for his works were social criticism, literary criticism, and theology.

THE Christ-child lay on Mary's lap,
  His hair was like a light.
(O weary, weary were the world,
But here is all aright.)

The Christ-child lay on Mary's breast,
His hair was like a star.
(O stern and cunning are the Kings,
But here the true hearts are.)

The Christ-child lay on Mary's heart,
His hair was like a fire.
(O weary, weary is the world,
But here the world's desire.)

The Christ-child stood at Mary's knee,
His hair was like a crown,
And all the flowers looked up at him,
And all the stars looked down.

Birth of Christ

A primary theme of Rainer Maria Rilke's (1875–1926) volumes of poetry is the abandonment of ordinary life for the sake of a spiritual quest. His major works include the Duino Elegies *and* The Sonnets to Orpheus. *This selection is from* The Life of the Virgin Mary.

HAD you not simplicity, then how
should this befall you which illuminates the night?
The god, who thundered above the peoples, now
makes himself mild and comes in you to light

the world. Did you imagine him as greater?

What is greatness? Straightway through all matter
where he passes moves his downright fate.
Even a star has no such highway. See,
these kings are great.

They drag before your lap

treasures which they deem the very greatest,
and you're astonished at these gifts perhaps—
but see here in the foldings of your shawl
how he already has surpassed them all.

All amber that ships carry far away,
the golden ornaments and overcloying
spices stealing in the senses: yet
all these were fleeting things that made no stay,
and finally one has little but regret.

But—you will soon know it—He brings joy.

First Coming

Author of more than forty books for children, Madeleine L'Engle is best known for her award-winning series beginning with A Wrinkle in Time. *She also writes adult mysteries and poems. This work is from her book* A Cry Like a Bell.

GOD did not wait till the world was ready,
till . . . nations were at peace.
God came when the Heavens were unsteady,
and prisoners cried out for release.

God did not wait for the perfect time.
God came when the need was deep and great.
God dined with sinners in all their grime,
turned water into wine. God did not wait

till hearts were pure. In joy God came
to a tarnished world of sin and doubt.
To a world like ours, of anguished shame
God came, and God's Light would not go out.

God came to a world which did not mesh,
to heal its tangles, shield its scorn.
In the mystery of the Word made Flesh
the Maker of the stars was born.

We cannot wait till the world is sane
to raise our songs with joyful voice,
for to share our grief, to touch our pain,
God came with Love: Rejoice! Rejoice!

A Hymn on the Nativity of My Saviour

English poet and dramatist Ben Jonson (1572–1637) had his friend William Shakespeare as an actor in his major work Every Man in His Humour. *As was common in his time, he also wrote poems with religious themes.*

I SING the birth was born tonight,
The author both of life and light;
    The angels so did sound it.
And like the ravished shepherds said,
Who saw the light and were afraid,
    Yet searched, and true they found it.

The Son of God, the eternal king,
That did us all salvation bring,
    And freed the soul from danger:
He whom the whole world could not take,
The Word, which heaven and earth did make,
    Was now laid in a manger.

The Father's wisdom willed it so,
The Son's obedience knew no No,
    Both wills were in one stature;
And as that wisdom had decreed,
The Word was now made flesh indeed,
    And took on Him our nature.

What comfort by Him do we win,
Who made Himself the price of sin,
    To make us heirs of glory!
To see this babe all innocence,
A martyr born in our defence—
    Can man forget the story?

Him Who Dwells Beyond the Worlds

This selection is attributed to Saint Romanos, who lived in the sixth century.

HIM who dwells beyond the worlds
The Virgin bore today.
Him who bounds the universe,
    Earth shelters in a cave.
Angels above the shepherds high
    Sing His bounteous praise.
Wise Men, guided by a star,
    Pursue their eager way.
For unto us is born,
    A tiny child, God of Eternal Aeons.

Bethlehem blooms as Eden, now,
    Come, let us go and see.
In a hidden covert there,
    We'll find all pleasantry.
Deep inside that stony cave,
    Paradise itself shall be.
For there the bud of kindliness
    Has burst the arid waste.
For there a well has sprung
    Which David longed to taste
For there a Virgin bears a child
    Who Adam's thirst shall sate.
For unto us is born,
    A tiny child, God of Eternal Aeons.

Welcome to Earth

This selection is part of a popular hymn by Martin Luther (1483–1546), "Vom Himmel hoch." His own musical ability and his insistence on congregational participation in worship led Luther to compose and adapt many hymns.

WELCOME to earth, thou noble guest,
Through whom e'en wicked ones are blest!
Thou com'st to share our misery,
What can we render, Lord, to Thee!

Ah, Lord, who hast created all,
How hast thou made thee weak and small,
That thou must choose thy infant bed
Where ass and ox but lately fed!

Were earth a thousand times as fair
Beset with gold and jewels rare,
She yet were far too poor to be,
A narrow cradle, Lord, for thee.

For velvets soft and silken stuff
Thou hast but hay and straw so rough,
Whereon thou king, so rich and great,
As 'twere thy heaven, art throned in state.

Thus hath it pleased thee to make plain
The truth to us poor fools and vain,
That this world's honour, wealth and might
Are nought and worthless in thy sight.

Ah dearest Jesus, holy child,
Make thee a bed, soft, undefiled,
Within my heart, that it may be
A quiet chamber kept for thee.

That Holy Thing

George MacDonald (1824–1905), a Scottish author and devout Christian, wrote more than fifty-two volumes of poetry, fantasies, novels, and religious writings. This selection is from his still popular book Diary of an Old Soul.

THEY all were looking for a king
    To slay their foes and lift them high;
Thou cam'st, a little baby thing
    That made a woman cry.

O Son of Man, to right my lot
    Naught but thy presence can avail;
Yet on the road thy wheels are not,
    Nor on the sea thy sail!

My how or why thou wilt not heed,
    But come down thine own secret stair,
That thou mayst answer all my need—
    Yea, every bygone prayer.

Lo, How a Rose E'er Blooming

The original fourteenth-century text of this still popular German carol had twenty-two stanzas. In Germany roses were and are favorite flowers. Roses are prevalent in Christian art, frequently symbolizing the Virgin Mary or, as in this carol, Jesus.

LO, how a Rose e'er blooming
From tender stem hath sprung!
Of Jesse's lineage coming
    As men of old have sung.
It came, a floweret bright,
    Amid the cold of winter,
When half spent was the night.

Isaiah hath foretold it
    In words of promise sure,
And Mary's arms enfold it,
    A virgin meek and pure.
Through God's eternal will
    This child to her is given,
At midnight calm and still.

The shepherds heard the story
    Proclaimed by angels bright,
How Christ, the Lord of glory
    Was born on earth this night.
To Bethlehem they sped,
    and in the manger found Him,
As angel-heralds said.

This Flower, whose fragrance tender
    With sweetness fills the air,
Dispels with glorious splendor
    The darkness everywhere.
True Man, yet very God,
    From sin and death He saves us
And lightens every load.

O Saviour, Child of Mary,
    Who felt our human woe,
O Saviour, King of glory,
    Who dost our weakness know,
Bring us at length we pray
    To the bright courts of heaven,
And to the endless day.

A Child of the Snows

*G. K. Chesterton (1874–1936), a British journalist by trade, was considered a
master of the ballad form in poetry. This Christmas poem is a good example.*

THERE is heard a hymn when the panes are dim
    And never before or again,
When the nights are strong with a darkness long,
    And the dark is alive with rain.

Never we know but in sleet and in snow,
    The place where the great fires are,
That the midst of the earth is a raging mirth
    And the heart of the earth a star.

And at night we win to the ancient inn
    Where the child in the frost is furled,
We follow the feet where all souls meet
    At the inn at the end of the world.

The gods lie dead where the leaves lie red,
    For the flame of the sun is flown,
The gods lie cold where the leaves lie gold,
    And a Child comes forth alone.

In the Bleak Mid-Winter

Christina Rossetti (1830–1894) is the pseudonym of Ellen Alleyne, the prolific English poet whose famous older brother was the painter and poet Dante Gabriel Rosetti. Before her death in 1894, she was a candidate to be poet laureate of England. Her Christmas poems, especially this one, are considered her most popular.

IN the bleak mid-winter
    Frosty wind made moan,
Earth stood hard as iron,
    Water like a stone;
Snow had fallen, snow on snow,
    Snow on snow,
In the bleak mid-winter,
    Long ago.

Our God, heaven cannot hold him,
    Nor earth sustain;
Heaven and earth shall flee away
    When he comes to reign:
In the bleak mid-winter
    A stable-place sufficed
The Lord God Almighty
    Jesus Christ.

Enough for him, whom cherubim
    Worship night and day,
A breastful of milk,
    And a mangerful of hay;
Enough for him, whom angels
    Fall down before,
The ox and ass and camel
    Which adore.

Angels and Archangels
    May have gathered there,
Cherubim and Seraphim
    Thronged the air:
But only his mother
    In her maiden bliss
Worshipped the Belovèd
    With a kiss.

What can I give him,
    Poor as I am?
If I were a shepherd
    I would bring a lamb;
If I were a wise man,
    I would do my part;
Yet what I can I give Him—
    Give my heart.

Of Her Flesh He Took Flesh

When Gerard Manley Hopkins (1844–1889) entered the Jesuit order in 1868, he burned most of his poetry. Only the small body of verse that he saved, plus some poems written later, survived and were published after his death.

Of her flesh He took flesh:
He does take fresh and fresh,
Though much the mystery how,
Not flesh but spirit now
And makes, O marvelous!
New Nazareths in us,
Where she shall yet conceive
Him, morning, noon, and eve;
New Bethlems, and he born
There, evening, noon, and morn—
Bethlem or Nazareth,
Men here may draw like breath
More Christ and baffle death;
Who, born so, comes to be
New self and nobler me
In each one and each one
More makes, when all is done,
Both God's and Mary's Son.

The Heavenly Christmas Tree

Fyodor Dostoyevsky (1821–1881) was born and raised in Moscow, growing up in the shadow of the brutal murder of his father by his own serfs. His masterworks, Crime and Punishment *and* The Brothers Karamazov, *deal with the human need for penitence and obtaining salvation through suffering. This tragic Christmas tale is from Constance Garnett's translation of* An Honest Thief and Other Stories.

I AM a novelist, and I suppose I have made up this story. I write "I suppose," though I know for a fact that I have made it up, but yet I keep fancying that it must have happened on Christmas Eve in some great town in a time of terrible frost.

I have a vision of a boy, a little boy, six years old or even younger. This boy woke up that morning in a cold damp cellar. He was dressed in a sort of little dressing-gown and was shivering with cold. There was a cloud of white steam from his breath, and sitting on a box in the corner, he blew the steam out of his mouth and amused himself in his dullness watching it float away. But he was terribly hungry. Several times that morning he went up to the plank bed where his sick mother was lying on a mattress as thin as a pancake, with some sort of bundle under her head for a pillow. How had she come here? She must have come with her boy from some other town and suddenly fallen ill. The landlady who let the "corners" had been taken two days before to the police station, the lodgers were out and about as the holiday was so near, and the only one left had been lying for the last twenty-four hours dead drunk, not having waited for Christmas. In another corner of the room a wretched old woman of eighty, who had once been a children's nurse but was now left to die friendless, was moaning and groaning with rheumatism, scolding and grumbling at the boy so that he was afraid to go near her corner. He had got a drink of water in the outer room, but could not find a crust anywhere, and had been on the point of waking his mother a dozen times. He felt frightened at last in the darkness: it had long been dusk, but no light was kindled. Touching his mother's face, he was surprised that she did not move at all, and that she was as cold as the wall. "It is very cold here," he thought. He stood a little, unconsciously letting his hands rest on the dead woman's shoulders, then he breathed on his fingers to warm them, and then quietly fumbling for his cap on the bed, he went out of the cellar. He would have gone earlier, but was afraid of the big dog which had been howling all day at the neighbour's door at the top of the stairs. But the dog was not there now, and he went out into the street.

Mercy on us, what a town! He had never seen anything like it before. In the town from which he had come, it was always such black darkness at night. There was one lamp for the whole street, the little, low-pitched, wooden houses were closed up with shutters, there was no one to be seen in the street after dusk, all the people shut themselves up in their houses, and there was nothing but the howling of packs of dogs, hundreds and thousands of them barking and howling all night. But there it was so warm and he was given food, while here—oh, dear, if he only had something to eat! And what a noise and rattle here, what light and what people, horses and carriages, and what a frost! The frozen steam hung in clouds over the horses, over their warmly breathing mouths; their hoofs clanged against the stones through the powdery snow, and everyone pushed so, and—oh, dear, how he longed for some morsel to eat, and how wretched he suddenly felt. A policeman walked by and turned away to avoid seeing the boy.

There was another street—oh, what a wide one, here he would be run over for certain; how everyone was shouting, racing and driving along, and the light, the light! And what was this? A huge glass window, and through the window a tree reaching up to the ceiling; it was a fir tree, and on it were ever so many lights, gold papers and apples and little dolls and horses; and there were children clean and dressed in their best running about the room, laughing and playing and eating and drinking something. And then a little girl began dancing with one of the boys, what a pretty little girl! And he could hear the music through the window. The boy looked and wondered and laughed, though his toes were aching with the cold and his fingers were red and stiff so that it hurt him to move them. And all at once the boy remembered how his toes and fingers hurt him, and began crying, and ran on; and again through another window-pane he saw another Christmas tree, and on a table cakes of all sorts—almond cakes, red cakes and yellow cakes, and three grand young ladies were sitting there, and they gave the cakes to any one who went up to them, and the door kept opening, lots of gentlemen and ladies went in from the street. The boy crept up, suddenly opened the door and went in. Oh, how they shouted at him and waved him back! One lady went up to him hurriedly and slipped a kopeck into his hand and with her own hands opened the door into the street for him! How frightened he was. And the kopeck rolled away and clinked upon the steps; he could not bend his red fingers to hold it right. The boy ran away and went on, where he did not know. He was ready to cry again but he was afraid, and ran on and on and blew his fingers. And he was miserable because he felt suddenly so lonely and terrified, and all at once, mercy on us! What was this again? People were standing in a crowd admiring. Behind a glass window there were three little dolls, dressed in red and green dresses, and exactly, exactly as though they were alive. One was a little old man sitting and playing a big violin, the two others were standing close by and playing little violins, and nodding in time, and looking at one another, and their lips moved, they were speaking, actually speaking, only one couldn't hear through the glass. And at first the boy thought they were alive, and when he grasped that they were dolls he laughed. He had never seen such dolls before, and had no idea there were such dolls! And he wanted to cry, but he felt amused, amused by the dolls. All at once he fancied that some one caught at his smock behind: a wicked big boy was standing beside him and suddenly hit him on the head, snatched off his cap and tripped him up. The boy fell down on the ground, at once there was a shout, he was numb with fright, he jumped up and ran away. He ran, and not knowing where he was going, ran in at the gate of some one's courtyard, and sat down behind a stack of wood: "They won't find me here, besides it's dark!"

He sat huddled up and was breathless from fright, and all at once, quite suddenly, he felt so happy: his hands and feet suddenly left off aching and grew so warm, as warm as though he were on a stove; then he shivered all over, then he gave a start, why, he must have been asleep. How nice to have a sleep here! "I'll sit here a little and go and look at the dolls again," said the boy, and smiled thinking of them. "Just as though they were alive! . . ." And suddenly he heard his mother singing over him. "Mammy, I am asleep; how nice it is to sleep here!"

"Come to my Christmas tree, little one," a soft voice suddenly whispered over his head.

He thought that this was still his mother, but no, it was not she. Who it was calling him, he could not see, but someone bent over and embraced him in the darkness; and he stretched out his hands to him, and . . . and all at once—oh, what a bright light! Oh, what a Christmas tree! And yet it was not a fir tree, he had never seen a tree like that! Where was he now? Everything was bright and shining, and all round him were dolls; but no, they were not dolls, they were little boys and girls, only so bright and shining. They all came flying round him, they all kissed him, took him and carried him along with them, and he was flying himself, and he saw that his mother was looking at him and laughing joyfully. "Mammy, Mammy; oh, how nice it is here, Mammy!" And again he kissed the children and wanted to tell them at once of those dolls in the shop window.

"Who are you, boys? Who are you, girls?" he asked, laughing and admiring them.

"This is Christ's Christmas tree," they answered. "Christ always has a Christmas tree on this day, for the little children who have no tree of their own. . . ." And he found out that all these little boys and girls were children just like himself. Some had been frozen in the baskets in which they had as babies been laid on the doorsteps of well-to-do Petersburg people, others had been boarded out with Finnish women by the Foundling and had been suffocated; others had died at their starved mother's breasts (in the Samara famine), others had died in third-class railway carriages from the foul air; and yet they were all here, they were all like angels about Christ, and He was in the midst of them and held out His hands to them and blessed them and their sinful mothers. . . . And the mothers of these children stood on one side weeping; each one knew her boy or girl, and the children flew up to them and kissed them and wiped away their tears with their little hands, and begged them not to weep because they were so happy.

And down below in the morning the porter found the little dead body of the frozen child on the woodstack; they sought out his mother too. . . . She had died before him. They met before the Lord God in heaven.

Why have I made up such a story, so out of keeping with an ordinary diary, and a writer's above all? And I promised two stories dealing with real events! But that is just it, I keep fancying that all this may have happened really—that is, what took place in the cellar and on the woodstack; but as for Christ's Christmas tree, I cannot tell you whether that could have happened or not.

Choosing God

Mothers' Union is an organization based in London and Durham, England, and dedicated to the well-being of mothers, children, and families. Considered a pillar of the Anglican Church of England, Mothers' Union is frequently quoted in newspapers in support of family causes.

CHOOSING God,
Choosing to let your child be born in poverty
and of doubtful parentage
Choosing an occupied country with unstable rulers
Choosing the risk of his dying in a dirty stable
after a long journey by a pregnant teenager
Choosing to let him grow up poor, and in danger,
and misunderstood by those who loved him,
Choosing God
we doubt the wisdom of your choices then,
and we doubt them now,
while the rich are still full
and it is the poor who get sent empty away.
Help us, lest we in our anger or ignorance
choose to walk another way.

Let Us Sing Noel

Liturgist, musician, and Medical Mission Sister Miriam Therese Winter's work "Mass of a Pilgrim People" premiered at Carnegie Hall in 1967. She has recorded more than a dozen award-winning albums and written six books on worship. This selection is from her recent anthology, SONGLINES.

ANGELS appeared in dazzling light.
Their song proclaimed a holy night,
For God took flesh to dwell on earth
And sent a star to herald the birth,
And shepherds sang Noel.

Sing a song of jubilation,
Word made flesh for our salvation.
Love in a manger, come and see:
Hope inhabits history.
Oh, let us sing Noel. Let us sing Noel.

Soon from afar came sages to see,
With symbols of prosperity.
They left their gifts, and from that day
They lived their lives a different way,
And angels sang Noel.

What need have I of incense and gold
When the poor are hungry and sick and cold.
When those in need no longer lack,
And the wealthy know there is no going back,
The poor will sing Noel.

Look to the manger; what do you see?
Our God embracing poverty.
When all our selfish cravings cease,
And people cherish justice and peace,
Then all will sing noel.

Night More Than Starry Night

Andreas Gryphius (1616–1664) was a German poet and dramatist known for his baroque style of compositions.

NIGHT more than starry night! Night lighter than the day!
Night brighter than the sun wherein the light is born;
Which God, the light, who lives in light, chose as his own!
O Night which all days and nights now comfort may!

O joyous Night wherein our deepest woe and sorrow
And darkness deep and worldly plottings dire
And dread and fear of Hell and horror shall expire!
Heaven bursts, but no thunder strikes tomorrow.

The Maker of days and nights this night has come,
Time's realm and human body to assume,
Bequeathing both flesh and time to eternal bloom.
The mournful night, the black night of our sins,
Darkness of the sepulchre shall vanish in this night.
Night lighter than the day! Night more than starry night!

Of the Father's Love

Marcus Prudentius (348–413) was an eminent early Christian poet from Spain. By profession a magistrate, he converted to Christianity late in life and eventually entered a monastery. This hymn began as a portion of one of his Nativity poems and has evolved over centuries into a Christmas carol that is loved today.

Of the Father's love begotten
Ere the worlds began to be,
He is Alpha and Omega,
He the source, the ending he,
Of the things that are, that have been,
And that future years shall see,
Evermore and evermore.

Oh, that birth forever blessed,
When the virgin, full of grace,
By the Holy Ghost conceiving,
Bore the savior of our race,
And the babe, the world's redeemer,
First revealed his sacred face,
Evermore and evermore.

This is he whom seers in old time
Chanted of with one accord,
Whom the voices of the prophets
Promised in their faithful word;
Now he shines, the long expected;
Let creation praise its Lord
Evermore and evermore.

Let the heights of heav'n adore him;
Angel hosts, his praises sing;
Pow'rs, dominions, bow before him
And extol our God and King;
Let no tongue on earth be silent,
Ev'ry voice in concert ring
Evermore and evermore.

Christ, to thee, with God the Father,
And, O Holy Ghost, to thee,
Hymn and chant and high thanksgiving
And unwearied praises be:

Honor, Glory, and dominion,
And eternal victory
Evermore and evermore! Amen

Go to Bethlehem

Donna E. Schaper is a writer, minister, and social activist affiliated with the Massachusetts Conference of the United Church of Christ. Her book of Lenten meditations is entitled Calmly Plotting the Resurrection.

L ET us go now to Bethlehem and see this thing which has taken place" (Luke 2:15). Place our hopes on Bethlehem this season, O God. Convince us that small is victor over large, that we can find a lot in a little. Slow us down. Move us out of the fast lane. Let every plan we make contain the seed of your Son's birth so that when the silent night comes, we can know the song in its silence, the gift in giving gifts and the peace that passes understanding in the quiet of our hearts.

Let us go to Bethlehem to find him who brings the scattered home. Come softly to us in this season, O Jesus. Bring us home by your path. Open our eyes and ears that we may welcome the life you bring. Revive the desert places in us that we may yet blossom.

Let us go to Bethlehem to meet him who hears us when we have no words, no justifications, no excuses, only the thud of facts and gnawing memories, only the knowledge that too many tables are thinly laid and that we, too, are poor in ways that frighten us.

Let us go to Bethlehem to find the child who amazes us. Bethlehem—so small, so insignificant—it seems unlikely that you should use it for your grand purpose. But you sneak in there, holy child, so silently, almost unobserved. And if you can use Bethlehem, that means you can use us. Come into our quiet space and point us to the purposes you have for us. At your manger make sense of our lives.

Let us go to Bethlehem and see that our usual hopes are too small, that the pragmatism of this world is inadequate to grasp the things you have in mind. Make us wild in hope—that AIDS will be cured, that peace will blanket the earth, that we will find calm for our souls. Show us that we are not alone, that you are with us, that in your smallness we find all we truly need.

From *The Second Shepherds' Play*

In fourteenth-century England, mystery plays were a favorite form of entertainment for religious holidays. Most mystery plays were based on the Bible. Members of craft guilds would be performers. This excerpt is from scene 7 of The Second Shepherds' Play.

SCENE 7. The Stable at Bethlehem, Mary and the child Jesus. (This can be represented by a tableau behind gauze, or by shadows if desired; soft music of "Adeste Fideles.")

FIRST SHEPHERD:
Hail, thou comely and clean one! Hail, young child!
Hail, Maker, as I mean, from a maiden so mild.
Thou hast harried, I ween, the warlock so wild,—
The false beguiler with his team now goes beguiled.
    Look, he merries,
Lo, he laughs, my sweeting!
A happy meeting,
Here's my promised greeting,
    Have a bob of cherries!

SECOND SHEPHERD:
Hail, sovereign Saviour, for thou hast us sought!
Hail, noble nursling and flower, that of all things hast wrought,
Hail, thou full of gracious power, that made all from nought!
Hail, I kneel and I cower. A bird have I brought
    To my bairn from far.
Hail, little tiny mop!
Of our creed thou are the crop.
I fain would drink in thy cup.
    Little day-star!

THIRD SHEPHERD:
Hail, darling dear one, full of Godhead indeed!
I pray thee be near when I have need.
Hail, sweet is thy cheer. My heart would bleed
To see thee sit here in so poor a weed,
    With no pennies.
Hail, put forth thy dall (hand)
I bring thee but a ball,
Keep it, and play with it withal,
    And go to the tennis.

MARY:
The Father of Heaven this night, God Omnipotent
That setteth all things aright, his Son has he sent.
My name he named, and did light on me ere that he went,
I conceived him forthright through his might as he meant.
　　　And now he is born,
May he keep you from woe.
I shall pray him do so,
Tell it forth as ye go,
　　　And remember this morn!

FIRST SHEPHERD:
Farewell, lady so fair to behold
With thy child on thy knee.

SECOND SHEPHERD:
　　　　　　　　　　But he lies full cold.
Lord, it is well with me. Now we go, behold!

THIRD SHEPHERD:
Forsooth, already it seems to be told
　　　Full oft!

FIRST SHEPHERD:
What grace we have found!

SECOND SHEPHERD:
Now are we won safe and sound.

THIRD SHEPHERD:
Come forth, sing are we bound.
　　　Make it ring then aloft!

(They depart singing.)

Christmas

George Herbert (1593–1633) was an Anglican priest whose metaphysical poems have been described as love lyrics to God. This selection may be read as two separate reflections under one title: one of a wayfarer seeking accommodation in an inn; the second of shepherds, flocks, and suns, the Lord's birth requiring an eternal paean of praise.

ALL after pleasures as I rid one day,
My horse and I, both tired, body and mind,
    With full cry of affections, quite astray,
I took up in the next inn I could find.
There when I came, whom found I but my dear,
    My dearest Lord, expecting till the grief
    Of pleasures brought me to him, ready there
To be all passengers' most sweet relief?
O Thou, whose glorious, yet contracted light,
    Wrapt in night's mantle, stole into a manger;
    Since my dark soul and brutish is thy right,
To Man of all beasts be not thou a stranger:
    Furnish and deck my soul, that thou mayst have
    A better lodging than a rack or grave.

The shepherds sing; and shall I silent be?
    My God, no hymn for thee?
My soul's a shepherd too; a flock it feeds
    Of thoughts, and words, and deeds.
The pasture is thy word: the streams, thy grace
    Enriching all the place.
Shepherd and flock shall sing, and all my powers
    Out-sing the day-light hours.
Then we will chide the sun for letting night
    Take up his place and right:
We sing one common Lord; wherefore he should
    Himself the candle hold.
I will go searching, till I find a sun
    Shall stay, till we have done;
A willing shiner, that shall shine as gladly,
    As frost-nipt suns look sadly.

Then we will sing, and shine all our own day,
    And one another pay:
His beams shall cheer my breast, and both so twine,
Till ev'n his beams sing, and my music shine.

Part 3

Epiphany
To Fill the World with Light

May the simple beauty of Jesus' birth
summon us always to love
what is most deeply human,
and to see your Word made flesh
reflected in those whose lives we touch.
Based on the Roman rite, Second Sunday after Christmas

Introduction

The power of light over darkness is the theme of the festival of Epiphany—the time set aside by the church to celebrate the showing forth of God's glory. The Light of the World has come to conquer the forces of death and evil. The star that led the Magi to the manger reminds us forever of God's guiding love.

So the Gift is given, the Good News extolled, the Promise kept. And now the work of Christmas begins. How do we show appreciation? What does gratefulness look like in our ordinary, daily life if the mystery of the Word made flesh has truly touched us? The writers of the selections in part 3 offer us a rich variety of approaches to these questions. They define for us what Christmas means and how we might respond.

Light of the World

A creative and prolific liturgist, hymn writer, and composer, Miriam Therese Winter also travels widely to lead programs on liturgy and social justice.

LIGHT of the world,
we bow before You
in awe and adoration.
Bless us
and our simple faith
seeking understanding.
Epiphany means
manifestation,
lifting the veil,
revelation.
Reveal to us then
what we need to know
to love You,
and serve You,
and keep Your word
with fidelity and truth,
courage and hope,
this day and always.
Amen.

The Magi

An Irish poet reflecting the divine mystery in all things, William Butler Yeats (1865–1939) is considered one of the finest English-language poets of the first half of the twentieth century.

NOW as at all times I can see in the mind's eye,
In their stiff, painted clothes, the pale unsatisfied ones
Appear and disappear in the blue depth of the sky
With all their ancient faces like rain-beaten stones,
And all their helms of Silver hovering side by side,
And all their eyes still fixed, hoping to find once more,
Being by Calvary's turbulence unsatisfied,
The uncontrollable mystery on the bestial floor.

It Was the Arrival of the Kings

Writer and poet Christopher Pilling was head of the French department at Keswick School in England. He is the author of many works, including Snakes and Girls *and* Foreign Bodies, *from which this selection is taken.*

IT was the arrival of the kings
that caught us unawares;
we'd looked in on the woman in the barn,
curiosity you could call it,
something to do on a cold winter's night;
we'd wished her well—
that was the best we could do, she was in pain,
and the next thing we knew
she was lying on the straw
—the little there was of it—
and there was this baby in her arms.

It was, as I say, the kings
that caught us unawares. . . .
Women have babies every other day,
not that we are there—
let's call it a common occurrence though,
giving birth. But kings
appearing in a stable with a
"Is this the place?" and kneeling,
each with his gift held out towards the child!

They didn't even notice us.
Their robes trailed on the floor,
rich, lined robes that money couldn't buy.
What must this child be
to bring kings from distant lands
with costly incense and gold?
What could a tiny baby make of that?

And what were we to make of
was it angels falling through the air,
entwined and falling as if from the rafters
to where the gaze of the kings met the child's
—assuming the child could see?

What would the mother do with the gift?
What would become of the child?
And we'll never admit there are angels

or that somewhere between
one man's eyes and another's
is a holy place, a space where a king could be
at one with a naked child,
at one with an astonished soldier.

There were three things . . .

British writer G. K. Chesterton (1874–1936) supported the church's social philosophy of distributism, which advocated the redistribution of property without state interference. He wrote on many theological topics in essays, poems, and fiction.

THERE were three things prefigured and promised by the gifts in the cave of Bethlehem concerning the Child who received them; that He should be crowned like a King; that He should be worshipped like a God; and that He should die like a man. And these things would sound like Eastern flattery, were it not for the third.

Befana: An Epiphany Legend

Phyllis McGinley (1905–1978) won the Pulitzer Prize for poetry in 1961 for her book Times Three. *This selection is from* Merry Christmas, Happy New Year.

BEFANA, the Housewife, scrubbing her pane,
Saw three old sages ride down the lane,
Saw three grey travellers pass her door—
Gaspar, Balthazar, Melchior.

"Where journey you, sirs?" she asked of them.
Balthazar answered, "To Bethlehem,

For we have news of a marvelous thing.
Born in a stable is Christ the King."

"Give Him my welcome!"
Then Gaspar smiled,
"Come with us, mistress, to greet the Child."

"Oh, happily, happily would I fare,
Were my dusting through and I'd polished the stair."

Old Melchior leaned on his saddle horn.
"Then send but a gift to the small Newborn."

"Oh, gladly, gladly I'd send Him one,
Were the hearthstone swept and my weaving done.

"As soon as ever I've baked my bread,
I'll fetch Him a pillow for His head,
And a coverlet too," Befana said.

"When the rooms are aired and the linen dry,
I'll look at the Babe."

But the Three rode by.

She worked for a day and a night and a day,
Then, gifts in her hands, took up her way.
But she never found where the Christ Child lay.

And still she wanders at Christmastide,
Houseless, whose house was all her pride.

Whose heart was tardy, whose gifts were late;
Wanders, and knocks at every gate.
Crying, "Good people, the bells begin!
Put off your toiling and let love in."

In choosing to be born . . .

This reading is attributed to the Office of Readings, Roman rite, and to the writings of Peter Chrysologus, who lived in the fifth century.

IN choosing to be born for us, God chose to be known by us. He therefore reveals himself in this way, in order that this great sacrament of his love may not be an occasion for us of great misunderstanding.

Today the magi find, crying in a manger, the one they have followed as he shone in the sky. Today the magi see clearly, in swaddling clothes, the one they have long awaited as he lay hidden among the stars.

Today the magi gaze in deep wonder at what they see: heaven on earth, earth in heaven, humanity in God, God in humanity, one whom the whole universe cannot contain now enclosed in a tiny body. As they look, they believe and do not question, as their symbolic gifts bear witness: incense for God, gold for a king, myrrh for one who is to die.

There is a legend . . .

John Shea has taught theology at Loyola University, Chicago, and Saint Mary of the Lake Seminary while writing many books, especially books of faith stories. This selection is from Starlight: Beholding the Christmas Miracle All Year Long.

THERE is a legend that the Magi were three different ages. Gaspar was a young man, Balthazar in his middle years, and Melchior a senior citizen. When they approached the cave at Bethlehem, they first went in one at a time. Melchior found an old man like himself with whom he was quickly at home. They spoke together of memory and gratitude. The middle-aged Balthazar encountered a teacher of his own years. They talked passionately of leadership and responsibility. When Gaspar entered, a young prophet met him with words of reform and promise.

The three met outside the cave and marveled at how each had gone in to see a newborn child, but each had met someone of his own years. They gathered their gifts in their arms and entered together a second time. In a manger on a bed of straw was a child twelve days old.

The message of Christ talks to every stage of the life process. The old hear the call to integrity and wisdom, the middle-aged to generativity and responsibility, the young to identity and intimacy. The revelation accompanies us. We marvel at its richness and adaptability. To find Christ at any stage in our lives is to find ourselves.

Yet when all enter together—the young, the middle-aged, and the old—we find a deeper truth. No matter where we are in the life process, we are still children of God. We are newborn from the hands of God at every moment. Our dependency and indebtedness does not go away with maturity. There are many stages in the life of a human person, and each stage presents different struggles and opportunities. Yet at each stage there is a permanent child. When we go in separately, we know we are in different places and different times. When we go in together, we know that even though we are different we are the same.

He is the image . . .

Paul's Letter to the Colossians, chapter 1, verses 15–20, contains one of the earliest creeds of faith in the Incarnation.

HE is the image of the invisible God, the firstborn of all creation; for in him all things in heaven and on earth were created, things visible and invisible, whether thrones or dominions or rulers or powers—all things have been created through him and for him. He himself is before all things, and in him all things hold together. He is the head of the body, the church; he is the beginning, the first-born from the dead, so that he might come to have first place in everything. For in him all the fullness of God was pleased to dwell, and through him God was pleased to reconcile to himself all things, whether on earth or in heaven, by making peace through the blood of his cross.

From *The Story of the Other Wise Man*

This excerpt is from the 1902 edition of the classic tale by Henry van Dyke (1852–1933) The Story of the Other Wise Man. Artaban, the Median, sees the Star in the East and wants to follow the Magi priests to bring a gift to the King. He sells his home and all his belongings to purchase three jewels: a sapphire, a ruby, and a pearl. On his long journey to Bethlehem, he gives his first two jewels to needy persons and stays to help others, delaying his travels. After many years, he arrives in Jerusalem with his last jewel, a pearl. Van Dyke wrote in the preface to his work: "And now that [Artaban's] story is told, what does it mean? How can I tell? What does life mean? If the meaning could be put into a sentence there would be no need of telling the story."

ARTABAN joined company with a group of people from his own country, Parthian Jews who had come up to keep the Passover, and inquired of them the cause of the tumult, and where they were going.

"We are going," they answered, "to the place called Golgotha, outside the city walls, where there is to be an execution. Have you not heard what has happened? Two famous robbers are to be crucified, and with them another, called Jesus of Nazareth, a man who has done many wonderful works among the people, so that they love him greatly. But the priests and elders have said that he must die, because he gave himself out to be the Son of God. And Pilate has sent him to the cross because he said that he was the 'King of the Jews.'"

How strangely these familiar words fell upon the tired heart of Artaban! They had led him for a lifetime over land and sea. And now they came to him darkly and mysteriously like a message of despair. The King had arisen, but He had been denied and cast out. He was about to perish. Perhaps He was already dying. Could it be the same who had been born in Bethlehem thirty-three years ago, at whose birth the star had appeared in heaven, and of whose coming the prophets had spoken?

Artaban's heart beat unsteadily with that troubled, doubtful apprehension which is the excitement of old age. But he said within himself: "The ways of God are stranger than the thoughts of men, and it may be that I shall find the King, at last, in the hands of His enemies, and shall come in time to offer my pearl for His ransom before He dies."

So the old man followed the multitude with slow and painful steps towards the Damascus gate of the city. Just beyond the entrance of the guard-house a troop of Macedonian soldiers came down the street, dragging a young girl with torn dress and dishevelled hair. As the Magian paused to look at her with compassion, she broke suddenly from the hands of her tormentors, and threw herself at his feet, clasping him around the knees. She had seen his white cap and the winged circle on his breast.

"Have pity on me," she cried, "and save me, for the sake of the God of Purity! I also am a daughter of the true religion which is taught by the Magi. My father was a merchant of Parthia, but he is dead, and I am seized for his debts to be sold as a slave. Save me from worse than death!"

Artaban trembled.

It was the old conflict in his soul, which had come to him in the palmgrove of Babylon and in the cottage at Bethlehem—the conflict between the expectation of faith and the impulse of love. Twice the gift which he had consecrated to the worship of religion had been drawn from his hand to the service of humanity. This was the third trial, the ultimate probation, the final and irrevocable choice. Was it his great opportunity, or his last temptation? He could not tell. One thing only was clear in the darkness of his mind—it was inevitable. And does not the inevitable come from God?

One thing only was sure to his divided heart—to rescue this helpless girl would be a true deed of love. And is not love the light of the soul?

He took the pearl from his bosom. Never had it seemed so luminous, so radiant, so full of tender, living lustre. He laid it in the hand of the slave.

"This is thy ransom, daughter! It is the last of my treasures which I kept for the King."

While he spoke, the darkness of the sky thickened, and shuddering tremors ran through the earth, heaving convulsively like the breast of one who struggles with mighty grief.

The walls of the houses rocked to and fro. Stones were loosened and crashed into the street. Dust clouds filled the air. The soldiers fled in terror, reeling like drunken men. But Artaban and the girl whom he had ransomed crouched helpless beneath the wall of the Praetorium.

What had he to fear? What had he to live for? He had given away the last remnant of his tribute for the King. He had parted with the last hope of finding Him. The quest was over, and it had failed. But, even in that thought, accepted and embraced, there was peace. It was not resignation. It was not submission. It was something more profound and searching. He knew that all was well, because he had done the best that he could, from day to day. He had been true to the light that had been given to him. He had looked for more. And if he had not found it, if a failure was all that came out of his life, doubtless that was the best that was possible. He had not seen the revelation of "life everlasting, incorruptible and immortal." But he knew that even if he could live his earthly life over again, it could not be otherwise than it had been.

One more lingering pulsation of the earthquake quivered through the ground. A heavy tile, shaken from the roof, fell and struck the old man on the temple. He lay breathless and pale, with his gray head resting on the young girl's shoulder, and the blood trickling from the wound. As she bent over him, fearing that he was dead, there came a voice through the twilight, very small and still, like music sounding from a distance, in which the notes are clear but the words are lost. The girl turned to see if some one had spoken from the window above them, but she saw no one.

Then the old man's lips began to move, as if in answer, and she heard him say in the Parthian tongue:

"Not so, my Lord! For when saw I thee an hungered and fed thee? Or thirsty, and gave thee drink? When saw I thee a stranger, and took thee in? Or naked, and clothed thee? When saw I thee sick or in prison, and came unto thee? Three-and-thirty years have I looked for thee; but I have never seen thy face, nor ministered to thee, my King."

He ceased, and the sweet voice came again. And again the maid heard it, very faintly and far away. But now it seemed as though she understood the words:

"Verily I say unto thee, Inasmuch as thou hast done it unto one of the least of these my brethren, thou hast done it unto me."

A calm radiance of wonder and joy lighted the pale face of Artaban like the first ray of dawn on a snowy mountain-peak. One long, last breath of relief exhaled gently from his lips.

His journey was ended. His treasures were accepted. The Other Wise Man had found the King.

Christ Climbed Down

The United States' favorite beat poet, Lawrence Ferlinghetti, was born in New York City, but he gained his fame in San Francisco, where he founded City Lights, a bookstore and publishing house. This selection is from A Coney Island of the Mind.

CHRIST climbed down
from his bare Tree
this year
and ran away to where
there were no rootless Christmas trees
hung with candycanes and breakable stars

Christ climbed down
from his bare Tree
this year
and ran away to where
there were no gilded Christmas trees
and no tinsel Christmas trees
and no tinfoil Christmas trees
and no pink plastic Christmas trees
and no gold Christmas trees
and no black Christmas trees
and no powderblue Christmas trees
hung with electric candles
and encircled by tin electric trains
and clever cornball relatives

Christ climbed down
from his bare Tree
this year
and ran away to where
no intrepid Bible salesmen
covered the territory
in two-tone cadillacs
and where no Sears Roebuck creches
complete with plastic babe in manger
arrived by parcel post
the babe by special delivery
and where no televisioned Wise Men
praised the Lord Calvert Whiskey

Christ climbed down
from his bare Tree
this year
and ran away to where
no fat handshaking stranger
in a red flannel suit
and a fake white beard
went around passing himself off
as some sort of North Pole saint
crossing the desert to Bethlehem
Pennsylvania
in a Volkswagen sled
drawn by rollicking Adirondack reindeer
with German names
and bearing sacks of Humble Gifts
from Saks Fifth Avenue
for everybody's imagined Christ child

Christ climbed down
from his bare Tree
this year
and ran away to where
no Bing Crosby carolers
groaned of a tight Christmas
and where no Radio City angels
iceskated wingless
thru a winter wonderland
into a jinglebell heaven
daily at 8:30
with Midnight Mass matinees

Christ climbed down
from his bare Tree
this year
and softly stole away into
some anonymous soul
He waits again
an unimaginable
and impossibly
Immaculate Reconception
the very craziest
of Second Comings.

Word Made Flesh

British scholar and poet Kathleen Raine specializes in studies of the metaphysical artist and poet William Blake. Her poetry collection The Holow Hill and Other Poems *is her best-known work.*

WORD whose breath is the world-circling atmosphere,
Word that utters the world that turns the wind,
Word that articulates the bird that speeds upon the air,

Word that blazes out the trumpet of the sun,
Whose silence is the violin-music of the stars,
Whose melody is the dawn, and harmony the night,

Word traced in water of lakes, and light on water,
Light on still water, moving water, waterfall
And water colours of cloud, of dew, of spectral rain,

Word inscribed on stone, mountain range upon range of stone,
Word that is fire of the sun and fire within
Order of atoms, crystalline symmetry,

Grammar of five-fold rose and six-fold lily,
Spiral of leaves on a bough, helix of shells,
Rotation of twining plants on axes of darkness and light,

Instinctive wisdom of fish and lion and ram,
Rhythm of generation in flagellate and fern,
Flash of fin, beat of wing, heartbeat, beat of the dance,

Hieroglyph in whose exact precision is defined
Feather and insect-wing, refraction of multiple eyes,
Eyes of the creatures, oh myriadfold vision of the world,

Statement of mystery, how shall we name
A spirit clothed in world, a world made man?

Immanence

Evelyn Underhill's (1871–1941) book Mysticism *has become a classic text. She was a leader and counselor to Anglican communities in England, she lectured on the philosophy of religion at Manchester College, Oxford, and she wrote many books and poems.*

I COME in the little things,
Saith the Lord:
Not borne on the morning wings
Of majesty, but I have set My Feet
Amidst the delicate and bladed wheat
That springs triumphant in the furrowed sod.
There do I dwell, in weakness and in power;
Not broken or divided, saith our God!
In your strait garden plot I come to flower:
About your porch My Vine
Meek, fruitful, doth entwine;
Waits, at the threshold, Love's appointed hour.
I come in the little things,
Saith the Lord:
Yea! on the lancing wings
Of eager birds, the softly pattering feet
Of furred and gentle beasts, I come to meet
Your hard and wayward heart. In brown bright eyes
That peep from out the brake, I stand confest.
On every nest
Where feathery Patience is content to brood
And leaves her pleasure for the high emprise
Of motherhood—
There doth My Godhead rest.
I come in the little things,
Saith the Lord:
My starry wings
I do forsake,
Love's highway of humility to take:

Meekly I fit my stature to your need.
In beggar's part
About your gates I shall not cease to plead—
As man, to speak with man—
Till by such art
I shall achieve My Immemorial Plan,
Pass the low lintel of the human heart.

In the middle of the night . . .

Dom Helder Camara is the archbishop of Olinda and Recife in Northeast Brazil, one of the poorest and least developed parts of the country. He writes poetry during nightly vigils. This selection is from It's Midnight, Lord.

IN the middle of the night,
When stark night was darkest,
then You chose to come.

God's resplendent first-born
sent to make us one.

The voice of doom protest:
"All these words about justice,
love and peace—
all these naive words
will buckle beneath the weight of a reality
which is brutal and bitter, ever more bitter."
It is true, Lord, it is midnight upon the earth,
moonless night and starved of stars.
But can we forget that You,
the Son of God,
chose to be born precisely at midnight?

It can and must be possible . . .

A poet, a musician, a Dutch minister of education, and a theologian and philosopher, the teaching field of the versatile Gerardus van der Leeuw (1890–1950) was the history of religion at the University of Groningen in Amsterdam. This selection is from his much translated work Sacred and Profane Beauty: The Holy in Art.

IT can and must be possible to recognize in the beautiful work of man the features of the work of God, since God himself gave to his earthly creation the features of his own image. It can and must be possible to praise the whole variety of the human world, the glorious multitude of forms of art and religion as revelation of the glory of God, if God himself gave himself to this human world, himself assumed form and moved as man among men. The Incarnation means our redemption, also in the sense that the world and our works in it need not be without meaning, but can be bearers of a divine revelation. . . .

Thus, as religious men, we experience again and again the miracle of the blending of religion and art. As theologians, who can neither separate artificially the revelation in Christ and that apparently different one given us as revelation, nor desire to lose ourselves in the generality of an idea of God, we find the unity of art and religion where alone we know unity: in the doctrine of the Incarnation. As believers, we find the possibility of complete beauty in him in whom we find everything, in the divine figure, in the son of Mary, in the Son of God, who is the most beautiful. And, with the old folk song, we say:

All the beauty
Of heaven and earth
Is contained in Thee alone.

Who Would Think

Members of the Iona community work and worship in a tenth-century abbey on the remote island of Iona, Scotland. They write many hymns and songs collaboratively in celebration of church festivals as well as for the seasons of the church year. This selection is for Christmas and is usually sung to the tune of "Scarlet Ribbons."

WHO would think that what was needed
    to transform and save the earth
    might not be a plan or army
    proud in purpose, proved in worth?
Who would think, despite derision,
    that a child should lead the way?
God surprises earth with heaven,
    coming here on Christmas Day.

Shepherds watch and sages wonder,
    monarchs scorn and angels sing:
    such a place as none would reckon
    hosts a holy, helpless thing;
Stabled beasts and passing strangers
    watch a baby laid in hay:
God surprises earth with heaven,
    coming here on Christmas Day.

Centuries of skill and science
    span the past from which we move,
    yet experience questions whether
    with such progress we improve.
In our search for sense and meaning,
    lest our hopes and humor fray,
God surprises earth with heaven,
    coming here on Christmas Day.

Christmas in a German Prison

Bishop Hanns Lilje (1899–1977) of Germany, a member of the underground Confessional Church in Germany during the Nazi era, was arrested on suspicion of playing a part in plots against Hitler. At the end of World War II, Lilje became widely known for his public confession of sins on behalf of the German people for their participation in war crimes. He also was known for his leadership in the world church in postwar missions for peace and refugee relief. This selection is taken from one of his books, entitled The Valley of the Shadow.

CHRISTMAS was near. Christmas Eve in prison is so terrible because a wave of sentimentality passes through the gloomy building. Everyone thinks of his own loved ones, for whom he is longing; everyone suffers because he doesn't know how they will be celebrating the Festival of Divine and Human Love. Recollections of childhood come surging back, almost overwhelming some, especially those who are condemned to death, and who cannot help looking back at their past lives.

It is no accident that in prison suicide attempts are particularly numerous on this special day; in our case, however, the most remarkable thing was the sentimental softness which came over our guards. Most of these S.S. men were young fellows, who were usually unnecessarily brutal in their behaviour, but when Christmas Eve came we hardly knew them—the spirit of this evening made such a deep impression upon them.

At this time we had a Commandant who was human. Although he had risen from the lower ranks to be an S.S. officer, he had remained an honest man, who, although he was harsh, was not brutal, and who often granted us certain facilities, until, on account of his humane attitude, he was removed from his post. Essentially he made more impression on us than his successor, who, in many respects, was also a decent man.

On this particular evening in the year, this Commandant had made various kind and humane actions possible; for instance, among us there was one who was condemned to death, and was already chained. The Commandant had his chains removed, and his violin was given back to him. This man was a great artist, and his playing was like magic. Presently the great vaulted Hall resounded with the beautiful strains of his violin.

As evening fell, I was walking up and down my cell, looking at a Nativity Scene which one of my children had made for me; illuminated by a candle, and decorated with some fir branches, it made my cell look like Christmas. Meanwhile I was thinking about the Christmas Eve service which I had conducted a year before in our Johanneskirche in Lichterfelde. It had been a memorable Christmas: a Christmas festival almost entirely without children, for most families had sent their children away from the city, since it was increasingly exposed to air raids. So the men who were left were chiefly men detained in Berlin by their war duties; or else they were older people, many of them solitary, who were rather indifferent to the dangers of air raids, and did not need to take care of themselves for the sake of other people. In any case, it was a remarkable congregation which gathered in the damaged, ice-cold church for the service on Christmas Eve.

As I recalled the service I remembered that I had preached on the words from the Prophet Isaiah: "The people that walked in darkness have seen a great light." At the beginning of my sermon, I had pointed out that when we were children we used to dawdle home after the Christmas service, because we wanted to look into everybody's windows to see them lighting up their Christmas trees, until at last we reached our own home, and stood spellbound before our own dazzling Christmas tree.

This year, however, all the windows were darkened, and the whole world was "blacked out." Then I said: "This year, we older people, men separated from their families, solitary people, old people, must learn to celebrate Christmas apart from all childish romanticism and all sentimentality, for this year there is no room for this sort of thing"; then, with the help of this prophetic saying, I tried to make clear the real meaning of the Christmas message for ourselves, grown-up people passing through a dark and difficult time.

I had just reached this point in my reflections, and had just begun to feel a painful longing for a congregation, to whom I might preach the Christmas Gospel on this very evening, at this hard and difficult time, when suddenly, outside my door, I heard my number called. Usually when this call resounded through the wing of our prison it didn't mean anything good. Too often it meant interrogations, or ill-treatment, removal from the prison, or still worse, but although I was prepared for anything, I really couldn't imagine that they would do something terrible to me; I rose, and followed the guard who led me downstairs from my cell in the third storey.

I was taken directly to the Commandant. In accordance with his usual custom he did not speak, but went on ahead to another cell. Before he entered this cell he turned to the guard, and said: "Bring number 212 to this cell too!" When the heavy cell door was opened a man rose to meet us; at once I saw in him a striking family likeness, and realized that he was Count X. His brother, one of the first to be condemned after the 20th of July (attempt on Hitler's life), had asked, just before his execution, that I might be allowed to give him the Sacrament, a request that was naturally refused. He had been one of the most frequent attenders at my services, and on the Sunday before his arrest he had joined in divine worship and had received Holy Communion.

Quite spontaneously, forgetting where I was, I mentioned this recollection to X, but the Commandant interrupted me harshly, saying: "I have not brought you gentlemen together for personal conversation!" Then he added, turning to the Count, "You asked that a certain clergyman, your own friend, might be allowed to visit you this evening in a pastoral capacity. Unfortunately I have not been able to accede to this request, but here is Dr. Lilje, who will address some words to you."

Now I saw what was expected of me. The Count replied: "What I really want, sir, is to make my confession, and then receive Holy Communion." Immediately I said that I was ready to do what was required; and the Commandant seemed to have no objection. So a small silver cup was brought, a little wine, and some bread—in the meantime number 212 had also been brought into the cell. He was the violinist who was under sentence of death. The guard was sent out of the cell, so we four men were there together.

At the Commandant's suggestion the violinist played a Christmas chorale, exquisitely; then, in this cell, and before this congregation, I read the Gospel for Christmas Day: "Now it came to pass in those days there went out a decree. . . ." The violinist played another Christmas chorale; in the meantime I had been able to arrange my thoughts a little about the passage in Isaiah which had filled my mind when I was summoned downstairs.

I said to my fellow prisoners: "This evening we are a congregation, part of the Church of Christ, and this great word of divine promise is as true for us today as it was for those of a year ago, among whom, at that time, was your own brother—and for all who this year receive it in faith. Our chief concern, now," I said, "is to re-ceive this promise in firm faith, and to believe that God, through Jesus Christ, has allowed the eternal light to 'arise and shine' upon this world which is plunged in the darkness of death, and that He will also make this Light to shine for us. At this moment, in our cells, we have practically nothing that makes the Christmas festival so familiar and so lovely, but there is one thing left to us: God's great promise. Let us cling to this promise, and to Him, in the midst of the darkness. Here and now, in the midst of the uncertainty of our prison life, in the shadow of death, we will praise Him by a firm and unshaken faith in His Word, which is addressed to us."

Then, in the midst of the cell, the Count knelt down upon the hard stone floor, and while I prayed aloud the beautiful old prayer of confession from Thomas à Kempis (which he himself had chosen) and then pronounced absolution, the tears were running silently down his cheeks. It was a very quiet celebration of the Sacrament full of deep confidence in God; almost palpably the wings of the Divine Mercy hovered over us, as we knelt at the altar in a prison cell on Christmas Eve. We were prisoners, in the power of the Gestapo—in Berlin. But the peace of God enfolded us: it was real and present, 'like a Hand laid gently upon us.'

Since the Commandant had obviously done all this without permission, and on his own personal responsibility, he could not al-low any further conversation. The violinist played a closing chorale; I parted from my fellow-prisoner with a warm handshake, saying: "God bless you, brother X." When we reached the corridor the Commandant shook my hand twice, with an iron grip; he was deep-ly moved; turning to me, he said: "Thank you! You cannot imagine what you have done for me this evening, in my sad and difficult dai-ly work."

I was immediately taken back to my cell, but I praised God, and indeed, I praised Him from my whole heart that in this building, under the shadow of death, and in the face of so much trouble and distress, a Christian congregation had assembled to celebrate Christ-mas. For it is possible to have every external sign of festivity and comfort and joyful celebrations, and yet not to have a true Christ-mas congregation, while in the shadow of death and in much trou-ble of heart a real Christian congregation can gather at Christmas.

It is possible for the candles and the lights to blind our eyes, so that we can no longer see the essential element in Christmas; but the people who "waited in darkness" can perhaps see it better than all who see only the lights of earth.

Upon us shines the Eternal Light,
Filling the world with radiance bright.

Shortly after Christmas, Count X was sent to a concentration camp. The violinist was killed by the Gestapo during the last days before the collapse; I have completely lost sight of the Commandant who, soon after this, was removed from his post because he had proved too humane. But the memory of my Christmas service in 1944, illuminated by the consoling and eternal Light of God, still remains with me.

Jesus

Although best known for her Lord Peter Wimsey detective novels, English writer Dorothy Sayers (1893–1957) also wrote the popular BBC radio drama The Man Born to Be King, *a play cycle on the life of Jesus. Other writings about her Anglican faith include* Creed or Chaos? *from which this excerpt is taken.*

JESUS . . . was in fact and in truth, and in the most exact and literal sense of the words, "the God by whom all things were made." . . . He was not merely a man so good as to be "like God"—He was God . . . for whatever reason God chose to make man as he is— limited and suffering and subject to sorrows and death—He had the honesty and the courage to take His own medicine. Whatever game He is playing with His creation, He has kept His own rules and played fair. He can exact nothing from man that He has not exacted from Himself. He has Himself gone through the whole of human experience, from the trivial irritations of family life and the cramping restrictions of hard work and lack of money to the worst horrors of pain and humiliation, defeat, despair and death. When He was a man, He played the man. He was born in poverty and died in disgrace, and thought it well worthwhile.

If Some King of the Earth

This well-known writing from a pre-eminent Christian metaphysical poet, John Donne (1572–1631), becomes appropriate for Christmas reading with its profound description of God's mercy in coming to earth. It can be of immense comfort to those who are unhappy at this time of year.

IF some king of the earth
Have so large an extent of dominion,
    in north and south,
As that he hath winter and summer
    together in his dominions;

So large an extent east and west,
As that he hath day and night,
    together in his dominions;
Much more hath God
    mercy and judgment together.

He brought light out of darkness,
    not out of a lesser light;
He can bring thy summer out of winter,
    though thou have no spring.

Though in the ways of fortune,
    or understanding, or conscience,
Thou have been benighted till now,
    wintered and frozen,
    clouded and eclipsed,
    damped and benumbed,
    smothered and stupefied till now,

Now God comes to thee,
    not as in the dawning of the day,
    not as in the bud of the spring,
But as the sun at noon to illustrate all shadows,
As the sheaves in harvest to fill all penuries.

All occasions invite his mercies,
And all times are his seasons.

The telephone call . . .

Author of The Power of Positive Thinking, *preacher, and publisher of the mass-circulation* Guideposts *magazine for Christian living, Norman Vincent Peale (1898–1993) devoted his life to telling inspiring stories about the faith. This selection is an excerpt from "I Remember Three Christmases."*

THE telephone call to my father came late at night, and from a most unlikely place—a house in the red-light district of the city. The woman who ran the house said that one of the girls who worked there was very ill, perhaps dying. The girl was calling for a minister. Somehow the woman had heard of my father. Would he come?

My father never failed to respond to such an appeal. Quietly he explained to my mother where he was going. Then his eyes fell upon me. "Get your coat, Norman," he said. "I want you to come too."

My mother was aghast. "You don't mean you'd take a fifteen-year-old boy into a place like that!"

My father said, "There's a lot of sin and sadness and despair in human life. Norman can't be shielded from it forever."

We walked through the snowy streets and I remember how the Christmas trees glowed and winked in the darkness. We came to the place, a big old frame house. A woman opened the door and led us to an upstairs room. There, lying in a big brass bed, was a pathetic, doll-like young girl, so white and frail that she seemed like a child scarcely older than I was.

Before he became a minister, my father had been a physician and he knew the girl was gravely ill. When he sat on the edge of the bed, the girl reached for his hand. She whispered that she had come from a good Christian home and was sorry for the things she had done and the life she had led. She said she knew she was dying and that she was afraid. "I've been so bad," she said. "So bad."

I stood there listening. I didn't know what anybody could do to help her. But my father knew. He put both his big strong hands around her small one. He said, "There is no such thing as a bad girl. There are girls who act badly sometimes, but there are no bad girls—or bad boys either—because God made them and He makes all things good. Do you believe in Jesus?" The girl nodded. He continued, "Then let me hear you say, 'Dear Jesus, forgive me for my sins.'" She repeated those words. "Now," he said, "God loves you, His child who has strayed, and He has forgiven you, and no matter when the time comes He will take you to your heavenly home."

If I live to be a hundred, I will never forget the feeling of power and glory that came into that room as my father then prayed for that dying girl. There were tears on the faces of the other women standing there, and on my own, too, because everything sordid, everything corrupt was simply swept away. There was beauty in that place of evil. The love born in Bethlehem was revealing itself again on a dark and dismal street in Cincinnati, Ohio, and nothing could withstand it. Nothing.

So that was the gift I received that Christmas, the frankincense knowledge that there is good in all people, even the sad and the forlorn, and that no one need be lost because of past mistakes.

Father of Our Lord

This selection is based on the Roman rite, Second Sunday after Christmas, from A Christmas Sourcebook, *Archdiocese of Chicago.*

FATHER of our Lord Jesus Christ,
    our glory is to stand before the world
    as your own sons and daughters.
May the simple beauty of Jesus' birth
    summon us always to love
    what is most deeply human,
and to see your Word made flesh
reflected in those whose lives we touch.

A Candlemas Dialogue

During the Crimean War, English poet Christina Rossetti (1830–1894) served as a nurse under Florence Nightingale. She was part of the Oxford movement to turn the Church of England back to its Roman Catholic roots. Several of her works take the form of a dialog with God.

LOVE brought Me down: and cannot love make thee
  Carol for joy to Me?
Hear cheerful robin carol from his tree,
Who owes not half to Me
I won for thee."

"Yea, Lord, I hear his carol's wordless voice;
And well may he rejoice
Who hath not heard of death's discordant noise.
So might I too rejoice
With such a voice."

*"True, thou hast compassed death: but hast not thou
The tree of life's own bough?
Am I not Life and Resurrection now?
My Cross balm-bearing bough
For such as thou."*

"Ah me, Thy Cross!—but that seems far away;
Thy Cradle-song to-day
I too would raise and worship Thee and pray:
Not empty, Lord, to-day
Send me away."

*"If thou wilt not go empty, spend thy store;
And I will give thee more,
Yea, make thee ten times richer than before.
Give more and give yet more
Out of thy store."*

"Because Thou givest me Thyself, I will
Thy blessed word fulfil,
Give with both hands, and hoard by giving still:
Thy pleasure to fulfil,
And work Thy Will."

Dream-Vision

Tillie Olsen has led the effort to get publishers to reprint the writing of women who had been forgotten. Author of the popular book Tell Me a Riddle *(also a movie) and other works, she has shown that stories of the ordinary and difficult lives of women can be redemptive. This selection is from* Mother to Daughter, Daughter to Mother.

IN the winter of 1955, in her last weeks of life, my mother—so much of whose waking life had been a nightmare, that common everyday nightmare of hardship, limitation, longing; of baffling struggle to raise six children in a world hostile to human unfolding—my mother, dying of cancer, had beautiful dream-visions—in color.

Already beyond calendar time, she could not have known that the last dream she had breath to tell came to her on Christmas Eve. Nor, conscious, would she have named it so. As a girl in long ago Czarist Russia, she had sternly broken with all observances of organized religion, associating it with pogroms and wars; "mind forg'd manacles"; a repressive state. We did not observe religious holidays in her house.

Perhaps, in her last consciousness, she *did* know that the year was drawing towards that solstice time of the shortest light, the longest dark, the cruellest cold, when—as she had explained to us as children—poorly sheltered ancient peoples in northern climes had summoned their resources to make out of song, light, food, expressions of human love—festivals of courage, hope, warmth, belief.

It seemed to her that there was a knocking at her door. Even as she rose to open it, she guessed who would be there, for she heard the neighing of camels. (I did not say to her: "Ma, camels don't neigh.") Against the frosty lights of a far city she had never seen, "a city holy to three faiths," she said, the three wise men stood: magnificent in jewelled robes of crimson, of gold, of royal blue.

"Have you lost your way?" she asked, "Else, why do you come to me? I am not religious, I am not a believer."

"To talk with *you*, we came," the wise man whose skin was black and robe crimson, assured her, "to talk of whys, of wisdom."

"Come in then, come in and be warm—and welcome. I have starved for such talk."

But as they began to talk, she saw that they were not men, but women:

That they were not dressed in jewelled robes, but in the coarse everyday shifts and shawls of the old country women of her childhood, their feet wrapped round and round with rags for lack of boots; snow now sifting into the room;

That their speech was not high flown, but homilies; their bodies not lordly in bearing, magnificent, but stunted, misshapen—used all their lives as a beast of burden is used;

That the camels were not camels, but farm beasts, such as were kept in the house all winter, their white cow breaths steaming into the cold.

And now it was many women, a babble.

One old woman, seamed and bent, began to sing. Swaying, the others joined her, their faces and voices transfiguring as they sang; my mother, through cracked lips, singing too—a lullaby.

For in the shining cloud of their breaths, a baby lay, breathing the universal sounds every human baby makes, sounds out of which are made all the separate languages of the world.

Singing, one by one the women cradled and sheltered the baby.

"The joy, the reason to believe," my mother said, "the hope for the world, the baby, holy with possibility, that is all of us at birth." And she began to cry, out of the dream and its telling now.

"Still I feel the baby in my arms, the human baby," crying now so I could scarcely make out the words, "the human baby, before we are misshapen; crucified into a sex, a color, a walk of life, a nationality . . . and the world yet warrings and winter."

I had seen my mother but three times in my adult life, separated as we were by the continent between, by lack of means, by jobs I had to keep and by the needs of my four children. She could scarcely write English—her only education in this country a few months of night school. When at last I flew to her, it was in the last days she had language at all. Too late to talk with her of what was in our hearts; or of harms and crucifying and strengths as she had known and experienced them; or of whys and knowledge, of wisdom. She died a few weeks later.

She, who had no worldly goods to leave, yet left to me an inexhaustible legacy. Inherent in it, this heritage of summoning resources to make—out of song, food, warmth, expressions of human love—courage, hope, resistance, belief; this vision of universality, before the lessenings, harms, divisions of the world are visited upon it.

She sheltered and carried that belief, that wisdom—as she sheltered and carried us, and others—throughout a lifetime lived in a world whose season was, as still it is, a time of winter.

My father . . .

Moss Hart (1904–1961) was a popular U.S. playwright during the 1930s and 1940s. He collaborated on hits such as Face the Music, The Man Who Came to Dinner, *and the Pulitzer Prize–winning* You Can't Take It with You. *This selection is from his book* Act One.

MY father was a bright and blooming ninety-one years of age now and I arrived in Florida with my wife to spend Christmas and New Year's with him.

On Christmas Eve we sat in his living room, and while my wife chatted with his nurse and companion, I sat on a sofa across the room with my father, showing him the pictures of his two grandchildren. Suddenly I felt his hand slip into mine. It was the first time in our lives that either of us had ever touched the other. No words were spoken and I went right on turning the pages of the picture album, but my hand remained over his. A few years before I might have withdrawn mine after a moment or two, but now my hand remained; nor did I tell him what I was thinking and feeling. The moment was enough. It had taken forty years for the gulf that separated us to close.

Oh, Love

*German mystic and ascetic Thomas à Kempis (1380–1471) was born of peas-
ant stock and entered an Augustinian monastery in Holland as an unexception-
al pious man. Yet he is believed to have written most of* Imitation of Christ, *a
highly influential Christian work, from which this excerpt is taken.*

OH, love, how deep, how broad, how high,
    Beyond all thought and fantasy,
That God, the Son of God, should take
Our mortal form for mortal's sake!

He sent no angel to our race,
Of higher or of lower place,
But wore the robe of human frame,
And to this world himself he came.

For us baptized, for us he bore
His holy fast and hungered sore;
For us temptation sharp he knew;
For us the tempter overthrew.

For us he prayed; for us he taught;
For us his daily works he wrought,
By words and signs and actions thus
Still seeking not himself, but us.

For us by wickedness betrayed,
For us, in crown of thorns arrayed,
He bore the shameful cross and death;
For us he gave his dying breath.

For us he rose from death again;
For us he went on high to reign;
For us he sent his Spirit here
To guide, to strengthen, and to cheer.

All glory to our Lord and God
For love so deep, so high, so broad;
The Trinity whom we adore
Forever and forevermore.

Christ speaks . . .

Saint Augustine (354–430) is remembered still today for his saying, "Our hearts are restless until they find their rest in Thee." This selection is from his writings after he became Bishop of Hippo in North Africa, four years after he was ordained a priest.

CHRIST speaks both in us and for us when, in one of the psalms, he says to the Father: I shall be satisfied when your glory is revealed. For he and the Father are one, and whoever sees him sees the Father also. . . . He will transform us and show us his face, and we shall be saved; all our longing will be fulfilled, all our desires will be satisfied.

But this has not yet been accomplished. . . . So while all this remains in the future and we still walk by faith, absent from the Lord, while we still hunger and thirst for justice and with inexpressible longing yearn for God's beauty, let us reverently celebrate the day he was born into our own servile condition.

Since we can as yet form no conception of his generation by the Father before the daystar, let us keep the festival of his birth of a virgin in the hours of the night. Since it is still beyond our understanding that his name endures for ever and existed before the sun, let us at least recognize his dwelling that he has placed beneath the sun. We cannot yet behold him as the only Son, abiding for ever in his Father, so let us recall his coming forth like a bridegroom from his chamber. We are not yet ready for the banquet of our Father, so let us contemplate the manger of Jesus Christ our Lord.

The birth of Christ . . .

John Shea is a gifted storyteller and writer of many prose and poetic works. His best-known works include Stories of God *and* The God Who Fell from Heaven. *This selection is from* Starlight: Beholding the Christmas Miracle All Year Long.

THE birth of Christ is the special celebration of the Christian peoples, but in a characteristic act of generosity its blessings are meant for all women and men. It is not meant for all people in the sense that they should become Christian. Expanding the membership of the Christian churches is not the same as being fed by the child. Neither is it meant for these people in the sense that if they do not "come to the manger," they will find neither God nor themselves. Arguing the exclusivity or uniqueness or superiority of Christ is not the same as saying this child fulfills a universal human promise. The birth of Christ is meant for all in the sense that the Christian revelation responds to an unavoidable human question, a search that arises wherever men and women wake up.

Of course, the search of awakened men and women may also lead them to Buddha or Mohammed or Krishna or Moses. We take help from wherever we can get it. We do not have to be an adherent of a religion to benefit from its revelation. We do not have to be a Taoist to learn from the *Tao Te Ching* or a Hindu to learn from the *Bhagavad Gita* or a Moslem to learn from the *Koran* or a Buddhist to learn from the *Dhammapada* or a Christian to learn from the Gospel of Luke. All we have to be is open. For the spiritual searcher the religions of the world are meant for the people of the world. As diverse as they are, as in need of criticism as they are, as in need of dialogue with one another as they are—they represent a cosmic revelation, "a ray of the truth which enlightens all human beings" [from Vatican II, "Declaration on the Relation of the Church to Non-Christian Religions," 28 October 1965, no. 2]. Therefore, all are invited to the birth of Christ and an angel in the night sky, even after he has calmed you down, is difficult to refuse: "I bring you glad tidings of great joy which is meant for *all* the people" (Lk. 2:10).

Dozens of exiles . . .

Famed storyteller, humorist, and host of public radio's A Prairie Home Companion, *Garrison Keillor has made Minnesotans and the fictional town of Lake Wobegon integral parts of Americana. This excerpt is from his book* Leaving Home.

DOZENS of exiles returned for Christmas. At Our Lady of Perpetual Responsibility, Father Emil roused himself from bed, where he's been down with cancer since Columbus Day, and said Christmas Eve Mass. He was inspired by the sight of all the lapsed Catholics parading into church with their unbaptized children, and he gave them a hard homily, strolling right down into the congregation.

"Shame. Shame on us for leaving what we were given that was true and good," he said. "To receive a great treasure in our younger days and to abandon it so that we can lie down in the mud with swine." He stood, one hand on the back of a pew, and everyone in that pew—children of this church who grew up and moved away and did well and now tell humorous stories at parties about Father Emil and what it was like to grow up Catholic—all of them shuddered a little, afraid he might grab them by their Harris-tweed collars and stand them up and ask them questions.

"What a shame. What a shame." They came for Christmas, to hear music and see the candles and smell incense and feel hopeful, and here was their old priest with hair in his ears whacking them around—was it a brain cancer he had? *Shame, shame on us.*

He looked around at all the little children he'd given first communion to, now grown heavy and prosperous and sad and indolent, but clever enough to explain their indolence and sadness as a rebellion against orthodoxy, a protest, adventurous, intellectual, which really was only dullness of spirit. He stopped. It was so quiet you could hear them not breathing. Then he said that this was why Our Lord had come, to rescue us from dullness of spirit, and so the shepherds had found and so shall we, and then it was Christmas again.

There Is Nothing I Can Give You

Fra Giovanni lived in the sixteenth century.

THERE is nothing that I can give you which you have not,
but there is much that, while I cannot give, you can take.

No heaven can come to us
unless our hearts find rest in it today.
Take Heaven.

No peace lies in the future,
which is not hidden in this present instant.
Take Peace.

The gloom of the world is but a shadow,
Behind it, yet within our reach, is joy.
Take Joy!

And so, at this Christmas time,
I greet you with the prayer that for you, now and forever,
the day breaks and the shadows flee away.

Little Joe stood outside . . .

Langston Hughes (1902–1967) demonstrated a varied writing talent in the forty years of his career, producing poetry, fiction, autobiography, journalism, drama, essays, translations, and works for children. This selection is an excerpt from "One Christmas Eve" in his book The Ways of White Folks.

L ITTLE Joe stood outside the ten-cent store in the light, and the snow, and people passing. Gee, Christmas was pretty. All tinsel and stars and cotton. And Santa Claus a-coming from somewhere, dropping things in stockings. And all the people in the streets were carrying things, and the kids looked happy.

But Joe soon got tired of just standing and thinking and waiting in front of the ten-cent store. There were so many things to look at in the other windows. He moved along up the block a little, and then a little more, walking and looking. In fact, he moved until he came to the white folks' picture show.

In the lobby of the moving picture show, behind the plate glass doors, it was all warm and glowing and awful pretty. Joe stood looking in, and as he looked his eyes began to make out, in there blazing beneath holly and colored streamers and the electric stars of the lobby, a marvellous Christmas tree. A group of children and grownups, white, of course, were standing around a big jovial man in red beside the tree. Or was it a man? Little Joe's eyes opened wide. No, it was not a man at all. It was Santa Claus!

Little Joe pushed open one of the glass doors and ran into the lobby of the white moving picture show. Little Joe went right through the crowd and up to where he could get a good look at Santa Claus. And Santa Claus was giving away gifts, little presents for children, little boxes of animal crackers and stick-candy canes. And behind him on the tree was a big sign (which little Joe didn't know how to read). It said, to those who understood, MERRY XMAS FROM SANTA CLAUS TO OUR YOUNG PATRONS.

Around the lobby, other signs said, WHEN YOU COME OUT OF THE SHOW STOP WITH YOUR CHILDREN AND SEE OUR SANTA CLAUS. And another announced, GEM THEATRE MAKES ITS CUSTOMERS HAPPY—SEE OUR SANTA.

And there was Santa Claus in a red suit and a white beard all sprinkled with tinsel snow. Around him were rattles and drums and rocking horses which he was not giving away. But the signs on them said (could little Joe have read) that they would be presented from the stage on Christmas Day to the holders of the lucky numbers. Tonight, Santa Claus was only giving away candy, and stick-candy canes, and animal crackers to the kids.

Joe would have liked terribly to have a stick-candy cane. He came a little closer to Santa Claus, until he was right in the front of the crowd. And then Santa Claus saw Joe.

Why is it that lots of white people always grin when they see a Negro child? Santa Claus grinned. Everybody else grinned, too, looking at little black Joe—who had no business in the lobby of a white theatre. Then Santa Claus stooped down and slyly picked up one of his lucky number rattles, a great big loud tin-pan rattle such as they use in cabarets. And he shook it fiercely right at Joe. That was funny. The white people laughed, kids and all. But little Joe didn't laugh. He was scared. To the shaking of the big rattle, he turned and fled out of the warm lobby of the theatre, out into the street where the snow was and the people. Frightened by laughter, he had begun to cry. He went looking for his mama. In his heart he never thought Santa Claus shook great rattles at children like that—and then laughed.

Santa Claus was a problem . . .

A humorist and the author of the "Observer" column for the New York Times, Russell Baker won Pulitzer Prizes in 1979 and 1983 for distinguished commentary. This selection is from "Observer," 18 December 1993.

SANTA Claus was a problem from the beginning, but I always liked him, and still do, and have no patience with people who don't. He brings fantasy and good feeling into our lives. These are valuable gifts these days when so few fantasies bring good feeling and so many take us down among the bleak and the monstrous.

From that early moment when reason first began to spoil for me the pure pleasures of existing, I tended toward skepticism about Santa Claus. It was not until the fevers of youth had subsided and I had passed beyond middle age's desperate struggle to pass for a grown-up that I fully escaped this glum skepticism.

It originated because the house in which I first became aware of being alive had no fireplace. Santa Claus, who delivered his goods by coming down chimneys, left some at my house despite its lack of a chimney.

Thus is the evil seed of skepticism planted in the unformed mind. I must have raised this question with an adult who told me that we did indeed have a chimney, which was the truth. To heat the parlor we used a woodburning stove. It was vented through a metal pipe which extended from the stove into the wall, conducting the smoke into a vertical shaft, which is to say a chimney.

Still, the physical improbability of a fat man in a red suit entering our front room through that metal pipe, barely nine inches in diameter, which even then would have left him trapped inside the wood-burning stove from which he would have to squeeze a corpulent figure and a bag of gifts—well, skepticism comes naturally to children with their primitive instinct for survival.

It takes a good deal of aging to outgrow it. It takes age's gift for reflection too. One day, if you have that, you interrupt your perpetual whining at the world long enough to reflect that in just simply having arrived here in this amazing wonder called life, you have been the beneficiary of miracles far more improbable than it would take to get Santa Claus through that metal pipe and out of our wood-burning stove.

As a child afflicted with reason, and therefore cunning, I did not express my skepticism to grown-ups. Cunningly I reasoned that since declarations of sour doubt might provoke a cutoff of Christmas goodies, a sensible person would keep his lip buttoned about his doubts and, instead, issue warm expressions of faith in this improbable delivery system.

Eventually, of course, puberty did its work, adolescence loomed on the horizon, and I was smitten by the terrible need to behave like a man of the world. In this long era when one year was ten years long and my knowledge expanded until it seemed there was nothing I didn't know—except how to stop blushing in the presence of girls—skepticism was the mire in which I wallowed.

Even then, however, Santa Claus retained power over me. Something about him made me feel—absurdly, inexplicably, nonsensically, irrationally—good.

I became aware of this strange power as a young man living in Baltimore, where one of the downtown department stores each year placed a laughing Santa Claus in a big window looking into the street. Life-size and remarkably lifelike, he sat on a throne of some sort, rocked ceaselessly from side to side and simply laughed, loudly and joyously.

Hour after hour the amplified roar of this laughter sounded through downtown Baltimore, drawing crowds to the window to investigate, then to be infected by the sound of it until it became impossible not to laugh with it.

The street was always packed with people standing there feeling as silly, I suppose, as I did about laughing and about feeling good for no sensible reason.

Soon after that I had to deal with the Santa Claus problem as a parent and did so by enthusiastically disengaging my children from any sensible adults who had mastered life's psychological pitfalls sufficiently to treat fantasy as dangerous to the young.

When our first-born was not quite two, I took her downtown to enjoy the excitement of that December's busyness and see the laughing Santa Claus. Alas, it was gone now, but I found a human Santa Claus in another shop window. "Santa Claus," I said to her. "Wave to him. Say hello." She smiled with utter credulity—without a trace of skepticism!—and said, "Hello, Santa Claus." What a beautiful memory it is.

Yes, Virginia

This famous letter and editorial response about Santa Claus first appeared over a hundred years ago, on 21 September 1897, in the New York Sun *newspaper. It has been translated into twenty languages. Editorial writer Francis Church was a highly regarded journalist and did not want the assignment to respond to little Virginia. Fortunately, he got it anyway.*

DEAR Editor: I am 8 years old. Some of my little friends say there is no Santa Claus. Papa says "If you see it in The Sun it's so." Please tell me the truth, is there a Santa Claus?—Virginia O'Hanlon, 115 West 95th Street.

Virginia, your little friends are wrong. They have been affected by the skepticism of a skeptical age. They do not believe except [what] they see. They think that nothing can be which is not comprehensible by their little minds. All minds, Virginia, whether they be men's or children's, are little. In this great universe of ours man is a mere insect, an ant, in his intellect, as compared with the boundless world about him, as measured by the intelligence capable of grasping the whole of truth and knowledge.

Yes, Virginia, there is a Santa Claus. He exists as certainly as love and generosity and devotion exist, and you know that they abound and give to your life its highest beauty and joy. Alas! how dreary would be the world if there were no Santa Claus! It would be as dreary as if there were no Virginias. There would be no childlike faith then, no poetry, no romance to make tolerable this existence. We should have no enjoyment, except in sense and sight. The eternal light with which childhood fills the world would be extinguished.

Not believe in Santa Claus! You might as well not believe in fairies! You might get your papa to hire men to watch in all the chimneys on Christmas Eve to catch Santa Claus, but even if they did not see Santa Claus coming down, what would that prove? Nobody sees Santa Claus, but that is no sign that there is no Santa Claus. The most real things in the world are those that neither children nor men can see. Did you ever see fairies dancing on the lawn? Of course not, but that's no proof that they are not there. Nobody can conceive or imagine all the wonders there are unseen and unseeable in the world.

You tear apart the baby's rattle and see what makes the noise inside, but there is a veil covering the unseen world which not the strongest man, nor even the united strength of all the strongest men that ever lived, could tear apart. Only faith, fancy, poetry, love, romance, can push aside that curtain and view and picture the supernal beauty and glory beyond. Is it all real? Ah, Virginia in all this world there is nothing else real and abiding. No Santa Claus! Thank God! he lives, and he lives forever. A thousand years from now, Virginia, nay, ten times ten thousand years from now, he will continue to make glad the heart of childhood.

O God, who . . .

A theologian at Union Theological Seminary in New York, William Adams Brown (1865–1943) also was involved in urban reform movements. He was one of the founders of the World Council of Churches and the author of The Quiet Hour, *from which this selection is taken.*

O GOD, who hast made us in Thine own image and given us the gift of thought that we may be able to understand the meaning of Thy handiwork and to use it aright, be with us now, we beseech Thee, as with reverent hearts and receptive spirits we draw near to Thee to receive the illumination we need. We thank Thee for every word Thou hast spoken to us and art speaking today, in nature, in history, in the Bible, through Thy Church, in the familiar experiences of every day. But most of all we thank Thee for Jesus Christ, the Word made flesh, through whom Thou hast translated all Thy other words into the language of life, and art drawing us to Thyself by the contagion of love. Help us to understand what we see in Him, interpret to us what we feel concerning Him. Be Thou our teacher as with expectant faith we seek to enter into the mind of Christ.

What has happened . . .

A most prolific and well-known English writer during his lifetime, G. K. Chesterton (1874–1936) was an outspoken critic of his country, openly wishing it were more like his ideal of Merrie Olde England. He hated modern puritanical dullness.

WHAT has happened to me has been the very reverse of what appears to be the experience of most of my friends. Instead of dwindling to a point, Santa Claus has grown larger and larger in my life until he fills almost the whole of it. It happened in this way. As a child, I was faced with a phenomenon requiring explanation. I hung up at the end of my bed an empty stocking, which in the morning became a full stocking. I had done nothing to produce the things that filled it. I had not worked for them, or made them or helped to make them. I had not even been good—far from it. And the explanation was that a certain being whom people called Santa Claus was benevolently disposed toward me. Of course, most people who talk about these things get into a state of some mental confusion by attaching tremendous importance to the name of the entity. We called him Santa Claus, because everyone called him Santa Claus; but the name of a god is a mere human label. His real name may have been Williams. It may have been the Archangel Uriel. What we believed was that a certain benevolent agency did give us those toys for nothing. And, as I say, I believe it still. I have merely extended the idea. Then I only wondered who put the toys in the stocking; now I wonder who put the stocking by the bed, and the bed in the room, and the room in the house, and the house on the planet and the great planet in the void. Once I only thanked Santa Claus for a few dolls and crackers, now, I thank him for stars and street faces and wine and the great sea. Once I thought it delightful and astonishing to find a present so big that it only went halfway into the stocking. Now I am delighted and astonished every morning to find a present so big that it takes two stockings to hold it, and then leaves a great deal outside; it is the large and preposterous present of myself, as to the origin of which I can offer no suggestion except that Santa Claus gave it to me in a fit of peculiarly fantastic goodwill.

Consider Jesus Christ . . .

A French mathematician and religious philosopher, Blaise Pascal (1623–1662) produced a monumental work, his thoughts—Pensees. Published after his death, these ideas continue to be read today.

CONSIDER Jesus Christ in every person, and in ourselves, Jesus Christ as father in a father, Jesus Christ as brother in a brother, Jesus Christ as poor in the poor, Jesus Christ as sovereign in princes, etc. For by his glory he is everything that is great, being God, and by his mortal life he is everything that is wretched and abject. That is why he took on this unhappy condition, so that he could be in every person and a model for every human condition.

In Christ . . .

Killed by the Nazis at the end of World War II for his leadership in the underground Confessional Church in Germany, Dietrich Bonhoeffer (1906–1945) had been able to write significant theological works prior to and during his imprisonment. This selection was quoted in Faith That Transforms.

IN Christ we are offered the possibility of partaking in the reality of God and in the reality of the world, but not in the one without the other. The reality of God discloses itself only by setting me entirely in the reality of the world, and when I encounter the reality of the world it is always already sustained, accepted and reconciled in the reality of God. This is the inner meaning of the revelation of God in the man Jesus Christ.

The whole concept . . .

This selection by writer Jane Vonnegut Yarmolinsky is from her book Angels Without Wings.

THE whole concept of God taking on human shape, and all the liturgy and ritual around that, had simply never made any sense to me. That was because, I realized one wonderful day, it was so simple. For people with bodies, important things like love have to be embodied. That's all. God had to be embodied, or else people with bodies would never in a trillion years understand about love.

Wonder as I Wander

Folk music came out of oral traditions among families and groups, and it belongs to the community, evolving in words and melody over time. This folk song came from the North Carolina countryside, a rich locale for such music through the nineteenth and early twentieth centuries, especially for songs that grew from the many religious revivals held there.

I WONDER as I wander, out under the sky,
How Jesus the savior did come for to die
For poor or'n'ry people like you and like I.
I wonder as I wander, out under the sky.

When Mary bore Jesus, 'twas in a cow's stall,
With wise men and an'mals and shepherds and all.
But high from the heavens a star's light did fall,
And the promise of ages it then did recall.

If Jesus had wanted for any small thing,
A star in the sky or a bird on the wing,
Or all of God's angels in heav'n for to sing,
He could sure have had it, 'cause he was the King.

I wonder as I wander, out under the sky,
How Jesus the savior did come for to die
For poor or'n'ry people like you and like I,
I wonder as I wander, out under the sky.

It is both terrible and comforting . . .

Karl Rahner's (1904–1984) theological works, written in his native Germany, continue to be important texts in both Roman Catholic and Protestant seminaries throughout the world.

IT is both terrible and comforting to dwell in the inconceivable nearness of God, and so to be loved by God that the first and last gift is infinity and inconceivability itself. But we have no choice. God is with us.

O Radiant Christ

Pastor, poet, and liturgist Ruth Duck was commissioned by the Lutheran School of Theology in Chicago to write this text in observance of an Epiphany vespers concert. She has edited a number of contemporary worship books, including Bread for the Journey and Sing a Womansong.

ORADIANT Christ, incarnate Word,
eternal love revealed in time:
Come, make your home within our hearts,
    that we may dwell in light sublime.

Our bartered, busy lives burn dim,
    too tired to care, too numb to feel.
Come, shine upon our shadowed world:
    your radiance bathes with power to heal.

Your glory shone at Jordan's stream,
    the font where we were born anew.
Attune your church to know you near:
    illumine all we say and do.

O Light of Nations, fill the earth;
    our faith and hope and love renew.
Come, lead the peoples to your peace,
    as stars once led the way to you.

As Shadows Cast by Cloud

Called a poet of nature, William Cullen Bryant (1794–1878) was a direct descendant of early New England Puritans and lived all his life in urban areas. First a lawyer, he later became a well-known newspaper editor in New York City just after the Civil War.

A S shadows cast by cloud and sun
Flit o'er the summer grass,
So, in Thy sight, Almighty One,
    Earth's generations pass.
And as the years, an endless host
    Come swiftly pressing on,
The brightest names that earth can boast
    Just glisten and are gone.

Yet doth the star of Bethlehem shed
    A lustre pure and sweet:
And still it leads, as once it led
    To the Messiah's feet.
O Father, may that holy star
    Grow every year more bright,
And send its glorious beams afar
    To fill the world with light.

By virtue of the creation . . .

A Jesuit and a paleontologist, Pierre Teilhard de Chardin (1881–1955) spent his life reconciling modern science and Christian theology.

B Y virtue of the creation and, still more, of the Incarnation, nothing here below is profane for those who know how to see.

From "In Memoriam"

Alfred, Lord Tennyson (1809–1892) was five years old when he wrote his first lyric at his rectory home in Lincolnshire. In 1850, after the death of a dear friend, he began a long series of elegies entitled "In Memoriam," which are excerpted here. The work recognizes that holidays can be reminders of lost loved ones. In 1850 Tennyson was named poet laureate of England.

28

THE time draws near the birth of Christ.
  The moon is hid; the night is still;
  The Christmas bells from hill to hill
Answer each other in the mist.

Four voices of four hamlets round,
  From far and near, on mead and moor,
  Swell out and fail, as if a door
Were shut between me and the sound;

Each voice four changes on the wind,
  That now dilate, and now decrease,
  Peace and goodwill, goodwill and peace,
Peace and goodwill, to all mankind.

This year I slept and woke with pain,
  I almost wished no more to wake,
  And that my hold on life would break
Before I heard those bells again.

But they my troubled spirit rule,
  For they controlled me when a boy;
  They bring me sorrow touched with joy,
The merry merry bells of Yule.

78

Again at Christmas did we weave
  The holly round the Christmas hearth;
  The silent snow possessed the earth;
And calmly fell our Christmas Eve.

The yule-log sparkled keen with frost,
  No wing of wind the region swept,
  But over all things brooding slept
The quiet sense of something lost.

As in the winters left behind,
　　Again our ancient games had place,
　　The mimic picture's breathing grace,
And dance and song and hoodman-blind.

Who showed a token of distress?
　　No single tear, no mark of pain:
　　O sorrow, then can sorrow wane?
O grief, can grief be changed to less?

O last regret, regret can die!
　　No—mixed with all this mystic frame,
　　Her deep relations are the same,
But with long use her tears are dry.

104

The time draws near the birth of Christ;
　　The moon is hid, the night is still;
　　A single church below the hill
Is pealing, folded in the mist.

A single peal of bells below,
　　That wakens at this hour of rest
　　A single murmur in the breast,
That these are not the bells I know.

Like strangers' voices here they sound,
　　In lands where not a memory strays,
　　Nor landmark breathes of other days,
But all is new unhallowed ground.

105

Tonight ungathered let us leave
　　This laurel, let this holly stand;
　　We live within the stranger's land,
And strangely falls our Christmas Eve.

Our father's dust is left alone
　　And silent under other snows;
　　There in due time the woodbine blows,
The violet comes, but we are gone.

No more shall wayward grief abuse
    The genial hour with mask and mime;
    For change of place, like growth of time,
Has broke the bond of dying use.

Let cares that petty shadows cast,
    By which our lives are chiefly proved,
    A little spare the night I loved,
And hold it solemn to the past.

But let no footstep beat the floor,
    Nor bowl of wassail mantle warm;
    For who would keep an ancient form
Through which the spirit breathes no more?

Be neither song, nor game, nor feast;
    Nor harp be touched, nor flute be blown;
    No dance, no motion, save alone
What lightens in the lucid East.

Of rising worlds by yonder wood.
    Long sleeps the summer in the seed;
    Run out your measured arcs, and lead
The closing cycle rich in good.

106

Ring out, wild bells, to the wild sky,
    The flying cloud, the frosty light;
    The year is dying in the night;
Ring out, wild bells, and let him die.

Ring out the old, ring in the new,
    Ring, happy bells, across the snow;
    The year is going, let him go;
Ring out the false, ring in the true.

Ring out the grief that saps the mind,
    For those that here we see no more;
    Ring out the feud of rich and poor,
Ring in redress to all mankind.

Ring out a slowly dying cause,
    And ancient forms of party strife;
    Ring in the nobler modes of life,
With sweeter manners, purer laws.

Ring out the want, the care, the sin,
    The faithless coldness of the times;
    Ring out, ring out my mournful rimes,
But ring the fuller minstrel in.

Ring out false pride in place and blood,
    The civic slander and the spite;
    Ring in the love of truth and right,
Ring in the common love of good.

Ring out old shapes of foul disease;
    Ring out the narrowing lust of gold;
    Ring out the thousand wars of old,
Ring in the thousand years of peace.

Ring in the valiant man and free,
    The larger heart, the kindlier hand;
    Ring out the darkness of the land,
Ring in the Christ that is to be.

The Incarnation, and Passion

Born into an aristocratic Welsh family and involved in the wars and political turmoil of his times, Henry Vaughan (1621–1695) became a major metaphysical poet after a dramatic religious conversion. Many of his writings focus on the experience of the divine.

LORD! when thou didst thy self undress
Laying by thy robes of glory,
To make us more, thou wouldst be less,
And becamest a woeful story.

To put on Clouds instead of light,
And clothe the morning-star with dust,
Was a translation of such height
As, but in thee, was ne'r expressed;

Brave worms, and Earth! that thus could have
A God Enclosed within your Cell,
Your maker pent up in a grave,
Life locked in death, heaven in a shell;

Ah, my dear Lord! what couldst thou spy
In this impure, rebellious clay,
That made thee thus resolve to die
For those that kill thee every day?

O what strange wonders could thee move
To slight thy precious blood, and breath!
Sure it was *Love*, my Lord; for *Love*
Is only stronger far than death.

For God so loved . . .

Why did God send Jesus to be born as a human being in Bethlehem? The answer is in this extract from the Gospel of John, chapter 3, verses 16–17 and 19–21, told in the eloquent simplicity of the version of the Bible commissioned by King James I in 1604.

FOR God so loved the world, that he gave his only begotten Son, that whosoever believeth in him should not perish, but have everlasting life. For God sent not his Son into the world to condemn the world, but that the world through him might be saved.

And this is the condemnation, that light is come into the world, and men loved darkness rather than light, because their deeds were evil. For every one that doeth evil hateth the light, neither cometh to the light, lest his deeds should be reproved. But he who doeth truth comes to the light, that his deeds may be made manifest, that they are wrought in God.

Loving Father . . .

Born in Edinburgh, Scotland, Robert Louis Stevenson (1850–1894) was an invalid most of his life. He became studious as a child and a writer as an adult. He is best known for Treasure Island, *but he also wrote poetry, including* A Child's Garden of Verse.

LOVING Father, help us remember the birth of Jesus, that we may share in the song of the angels, the gladness of the shepherds and the wisdom of the wise men.

Close the door of hate and open the door of love all over the world.

Let kindness come with every gift and good desires with every greeting.

Deliver us from evil by the blessing which Christ brings and teach us to be merry with clean hearts.

May the Christmas morning make us happy to be your children and the Christmas evening bring us to our beds with grateful thoughts, forgiving and forgiven, for Jesus' sake. Amen.

The Work of Christmas

A Baptist minister, Howard Thurman (1899–1981) became dean of Marsh Chapel, Boston University, before retiring to San Francisco and founding an interfaith, interracial congregation there. He is best known for his many books of devotions and social commentary.

WHEN the song of the angels is stilled.
When the star in the sky is gone.
When the Magi and elders are home,
When the shepherds are back with their flock.

The work of Christmas begins:
To find the lost.
To heal the broken.
To feed the hungry.
To release the prisoner.
To rebuild the nations.
To bring peace among all peoples.
To make music in the heart.

And now God says to us . . .

Karl Rahner (1904–1984), a German Jesuit, was a foremost Christian theologian of the twentieth century. He is known for his volumes entitled Theological Investigations. *A longer version of this selection came to storyteller John Shea in a Christmas card, and the text given here is as quoted in Shea's book* Starlight: Beholding the Christmas Miracle All Year Long.

A ND now God says to us what he has already said to the world as a whole through his grace-filled birth: "I am there. I am with you. I am your life. I am the gloom of your daily routine. Why will you not bear it? I weep your tears—pour out yours to me, my child. I am your joy. Do not be afraid to be happy, for ever since I wept, joy is the standard of living that is really more suitable than the anxiety and grief of those who think they have no hope. I am the blind alleys of all your paths, for when you no longer know how to go any farther, then you have reached me, foolish child, though you are not aware of it. I am in your anxiety, for I have shared it by suffering it.

This reality—incomprehensible wonder of my almighty love— I have sheltered safely in the cold stable of your world. I am there. I no longer go away from this world, even if you do not see me now. . . . I am there. It is Christmas. Light the candles. They have more right to exist than all the darkness. It is Christmas. Christmas that lasts forever.

Part 4

Praise
Joy to the World

Lord! and shall angels have their songs,
And men no tunes to raise?
O may we lose these useless tongues
When they forget to praise!
Isaac Watts (1674–1748)

Introduction

WHEN we are overwhelmed with gratefulness for the gifts of God, words are often inadequate. Dancing, shouting, and singing seem more appropriate, and they were the favored modes of expression at religious festivals in centuries past. Nineteenth-century hymn writer Robert Lowry captured this spirit in his lyric: "The peace of Christ makes fresh my heart, a fountain everspringing! All things are mine since I am his! How can I keep from singing?"

The following readings express some of the exuberant joy—in spite of life's tribulations—that comes to those who believe in the Christ of Christmas.

Christmas Carol

The son of former slaves, Paul Laurence Dunbar (1872–1906) was born in Dayton, Ohio. With the publication of his third book of poems, Lyrics of Lowly Life, in 1896, he became the first African American poet to win a national audience.

RING out, ye bells!
All Nature swells
With gladness of the wondrous story,—
    The world was lorn,
    But Christ is born
To change our sadness into glory.

    Sing, earthlings, sing!
    To-night a King
Hath come from heaven's high throne to bless us.
    The outstretched hand
    O'er all the land
Is raised in pity to caress us.

    Come at His call;
    Be joyful all;
Away with mourning and with sadness!
    The heavenly choir
    With holy fire
Their voices raise in songs of gladness.

    The darkness breaks
    And Dawn awakes,
Her cheeks suffused with youthful blushes.
    The rocks and stones
    In holy tones
Are singing sweeter than the thrushes.

    Then why should we
    In silence be,
When Nature lends her voice to praises;
    When heaven and earth
    Proclaim the truth
Of Him for whom that lone star blazes?

No, be not still,
    But with a will
Strike all your harps and set them ringing;
    On hill and heath
    Let every breath
Throw all its power into singing!

Rejoice and Be Merry

Rev. I. J. T. Darwall found this seventeenth-century carol by an unknown author in an old book in a church-gallery in Dorset, England, in the early part of the twentieth century. It appeared in the 1928 edition of The Oxford Book of Carols.

REJOICE and be merry in songs and in mirth!
O praise our Redeemer, all mortals on earth!
For this is the birthday of Jesus our King,
Who brought us salvation—his praises we'll sing!

A heavenly vision appeared in the sky;
Vast numbers of angels the Shepherds did spy,
Proclaiming the birthday of Jesus our King,
Who brought us salvation—his praises we'll sing!

Likewise a bright star in the sky did appear,
Which led the Wise Men from the east to draw near;
They found the Messiah, sweet Jesus our King,
Who brought us salvation—his praises we'll sing!

And when they were come, they their treasures unfold,
And unto him offered myrrh, incense, and gold.
So blessèd for ever be Jesus our King,
Who brought us salvation—his praises we'll sing!

The Praise of Christmas

The first two verses of this piece are by Tom Durfey (1653–1723), a dramatist and a friend of Charles II, in his Pills to Purge Melancholy.

ALL hail to the days that merit more praise
　　　Than all the rest of the year,
And welcome the nights that double delights
　　　As well for the poor as the peer!
Good fortune attend each merry man's friend
　　　That doth but the best that he may,
Forgetting old wrongs with carols and songs,
　　　To drive the cold winter away.

'Tis ill for a mind to anger inclined
　　　To think of small injuries now;
If wrath be to seek, do not lend her thy cheek,
　　　Nor let her inhabit thy brow.
Cross out of thy books malevolent looks,
　　　Both beauty and youth's decay,
And wholly consort with mirth and with sport,
　　　To drive the cold winter away.

This time of the year is spent in good cheer,
　　　And neighbours together do meet,
To sit by the fire, with friendly desire,
　　　Each other in love to greet.
Old grudges forgot are put in the pot,
　　　All sorrows aside they lay;
The old and the young doth carol this song,
　　　To drive the cold winter away.

When Christmas's tide comes in like a bride,
　　　With holly and ivy clad,
Twelve days in the year much mirth and good cheer
　　　In every household is had.
The country guise is then to devise
　　　Some gambols of Christmas play,
Whereat the young men do best that they can
　　　To drive the cold winter away.

Joy to the World

At an early age, Isaac Watts (1674–1748) showed an unusual talent for writing poetic verse. Because only psalms—God's actual words—could be sung in church, and ponderously at that, Watt's rector father suggested he write psalm hymns, which he did to great success. This beloved carol is based on Psalm 98.

JOY to the world, the Lord is come!
Let earth receive its King;
Let ev'ry heart prepare him room
And heav'n and nature sing, and heav'n and nature sing,
And heav'n, and heav'n and nature sing.

Joy to the earth, the Savior reigns!
Let all their songs employ,
While fields and floods, rocks, hills, and plains
Repeat the sounding joy, repeat the sounding joy,
Repeat, repeat the sounding joy.

No more let sin and sorrow grow
Nor thorns infest the ground;
He comes to make his blessings flow
Far as the curse is found, far as the curse is found,
Far as, far as the curse is found.

He rules the world with truth and grace
And makes the nations prove
The glories of his righteousness
And wonders of his love, and wonders of his love,
And wonders, wonders of his love.

The word "Carol" . . .

This selection is from the preface to The Oxford Book of Carols, *written by one of the book's editors, Percy Dearmer. His fellow editors on that collection of music and lyrics were R. Vaughan Williams and Martin Shaw. It was first published by Oxford University Press in 1928.*

THE word "Carol" has a dancing origin, and once meant to dance in a ring: it may go back, through the Old French *"caroler"* and the Latin *"choraula,"* to the Greek *"choraules,"* a flute-player for chorus dancing, and ultimately to the *"choros,"* which was originally a circling dance and the origin of the Attic drama.

The carol, in fact, by forsaking the timeless contemplative melodies of the Church, began the era of modern music, which has throughout been based upon the dance. But, none the less, joyfulness in the words has been sometimes discarded by those who were professionally afraid of gaiety. Some French carols were rewritten by well-meaning clergymen into frigid expositions of edifying theology; some of the English tunes were used by excellent Methodists of the eighteenth century to preach their favourite doctrines. Before their time the British tendency to lugubriousness had occasionally shown itself in the folk-carol: but even in such cases the dancing tunes remained, happily to belie the words; and in France behind the ecclesiastical propriety of modern noëls there lurk many carols like "Guillô, pran ton tamborin" (No. 82) to bear witness to the spirit of a more spontaneous and undoubting faith.

The typical carol gives voice to the common emotions of healthy people in language that can be understood and music that can be shared by all. Because it is popular it is therefore genial as well as simple; it dances because it is so Christian, echoing St. Paul's conception of the fruits of the Spirit in its challenge to be merry— "Love and joy come to you." Indeed, to take life with real seriousness is to take it joyfully, for seriousness is only sad when it is superficial: the carol is thus all the nearer to the ultimate truth because it is jolly.

So, on the one hand, the genius of the carol is an antidote to the levity of much present-day literature, music, and drama, made by men who are afraid to touch the deeper issues of life because seriousness is associated in their minds with gloom; for its jubilant melodies can encircle the most solemn of themes: on the other hand, it is an antidote to pharisaism, the formalism which is always morose, as Paul Sabatier says in his life of Francis of Assisi—that most Christian of saints, who as scenic artist at the Greccio crib, and as the sweet-voiced troubadour of the Holy Spirit, the "joculator Dei", was the precursor if not the parent of the carol. . . .

Carols, moreover, were always modern, expressing the manner in which the ordinary man at his best understood the ideas of his age, and bringing traditional conservative religion up to date: the carol did this for the fifteenth century after the collapse of the old feudal order, and should do the same for the twentieth. The charm of an old carol lies precisely in its having been true to the period in which it was written, and those which are alive to-day retain their vitality because of this sincerity; for imitations are always sickly and short-lived. A genuine carol may have faults of grammar, logic, and prosody; but one fault it never has—that of sham antiquity.

My Life Flows On

Robert Lowry (1826–1899), the pastor of Hanson Place Baptist Church in Brooklyn from 1861 to 1869, also was a publisher of church music, particularly Sunday school songs. He wrote the popular "Shall We Gather at the River" during an epidemic in his community.

M Y life flows on in endless song;
above earth's lamentation,
I catch the sweet, though far-off hymn
    that hails a new creation.

No storm can shake my inmost calm
    while to that Rock I'm clinging.
Since Christ is Lord of heaven and earth,
    how can I keep from singing?

Through all the tumult and the strife,
    I hear that music ringing.
It finds an echo in my soul.
    How can I keep from singing?

What though my joys and comforts die?
    The Lord my Savior liveth.
What though the darkness gather round?
    Songs in the night he giveth.

The peace of Christ makes fresh my heart,
    a fountain ever springing!
All things are mine since I am his!
    How can I keep from singing?

Words at the Solstice

Gordon Lathrop, a professor of worship at Philadelphia Lutheran Seminary, is coauthor of Lectionary for the Christian People, *an inclusive-language rendering of the Sunday Scripture readings for churches that follow this international guide. This reading is from his journal article "Christmas 1970: Words at the Solstice," in* Dialog, *fall 1982.*

TOMORROW shall be my dancing day.
I would my true love did so chance
To see the legend of my play
To call my true love to my dance.
Sing, O my love, O my love, my love, my love.
This have I done for my true love.

In a manger laid and wrapped I was,
So very poor, this was my chance,
Betwixt an ox and a silly poor ass,
To call my true love to my dance.

Christmas is an ancient feast of frivolity (the Puritans forbade it!) and this English carol seems to have caught that spirit, anticipating the current "theology of play." If we wish you a playful, dancing, merry Christmas our intention is not the hope that you will find some rough mockery of the ecstasy, the pattern, the joy and the grace of the Ancient Dance in the frenzied days, the harried attempts to make sense of our lives, the half-guilty celebrations, the stilted human relationships which mark our fasts and fill our days.

It is rather the hope that you may perceive the legend of God's play: "this have I done for my true love"—and that the festival of this prodigality will strengthen and deepen the elements of the Dance in your life: love and forgiveness and mystery and harmony and grace and attention and wonder and jubilation and praise and bodiliness and freedom and a *pas de deux* spontaneously discovered for a few moments or labored out over faithful years.

In this year of the plod and march of technology and war, of our own plod and march, we wish you the Dance of the Word of God. Now he shares our poverty and there is a chance.

I know nothing, except what everyone
knows—if there when Grace dances,
I should dance.

W. H. Auden

Everywhere, Everywhere, Christmas Tonight

Anglican bishop Phillips Brooks (1835–1893) was a poet as well as a great preacher in the United States. He refused to be drawn into controversy or to express intolerant opinions. His combination, in his preaching and writings, of a simple piety with intellectual clarity continues to be inspiring.

EVERYWHERE, everywhere, Christmas tonight!
Christmas in lands of the fir-tree and pine,
Christmas in lands of the palm-tree and vine,
Christmas where snow-peaks stand solemn and white,
Christmas where cornfields lie sunny and bright,
    Everywhere, everywhere, Christmas tonight!

Christmas where children are hopeful and gay,
Christmas where old men are patient and gray,
Christmas where peace, like a dove in its flight,
Broods o'er brave men in the thick of the fight
    Everywhere, everywhere, Christmas tonight!

For the Christ-child who comes is the Master of all,
No palace too great and no cottage too small;
The angels who welcome Him sing from the height,
"In the city of David, a King in His might."
    Everywhere, everywhere, Christmas tonight!

Then let every heart keep its Christmas within,
Christ's pity for sorrow, Christ's hatred for sin,
Christ's care for the weakest, Christ's courage for right,
Christ's dread of the darkness, Christ's love of the light,
    Everywhere, everywhere, Christmas tonight!

So the stars of the midnight which compass us round
Shall see a strange glory, and hear a sweet sound,
And cry, "Look! the earth is aflame with delight,
O sons of the morning, rejoice at the sight."
    Everywhere, everywhere, Christmas tonight!

Shepherds, Rejoice

Isaac Watts (1674–1748), considered to be the father of English hymnody, be-
came the minister of a Congregational church in London and wrote about six
hundred hymns, as well as many philosophical and theological works. Watts said
his hymns were "of human composure"—in everyday language—rather than
structured in stilted churchly phrases.

SHEPHERDS, rejoice, lift up your eyes.
And send your fears away;
News from the region of the skies!
Salvation's born today.

"Jesus, the God whom Angels fear,
Comes down to dwell with you;
Today He makes His entrance here,
But not as monarchs do.

"No gold, nor purple swaddling-bands,
Nor royal shining things;
A manger for His cradle stands,
And holds the King of kings.

"Go, shepherds, where the Infant lies,
And see His humble throne:
With tears of joy in all your eyes
Go, shepherds, kiss the Son."

Thus Gabriel sang; and straight around
The heavenly armies throng;
They tune their harps to lofty sound,
And thus conclude the song:

"Glory to God that reigns above,
Let peace surround the earth;
Mortals shall know their Maker's love
At their Redeemer's birth."

Lord! and shall angels have their songs,
And men no tunes to raise?
O may we lose these useless tongues
When they forget to praise!

Glory to God that reigns above,
That pitied us, forlorn!
We join to sing our Maker's love—
For there's a Saviour born!

Hark, the Glad Sound

Congregational minister Philip Doddridge (1702–1751) is ranked as a fine eighteenth-century English hymn writer, along with Isaac Watts and Charles Wesley. He wrote some four hundred hymns, including the still popular "O Happy Day."

HARK, the glad Sound! The Savior comes,
The Savior promised long;
Let ev'ry heart prepare a throne
And ev'ry voice a song.

He comes the pris'ners to release,
In Satan's bondage held.
The gates of brass before him burst,
The iron fetters yield.

He comes the broken heart to bind,
The bleeding soul to cure,
And with the treasures of his grace
To enrich the humble poor.

Our glad hosannas, Prince of Peace,
Your welcome shall proclaim,
And heav'n's eternal arches ring
With your beloved name.

The Incarnation

Charles Wesley (1707–1788) was the founder of the Methodist Society in England, and his brother John became the leader of the society in 1729. Charles wrote sixty-five hundred hymns at one count, including "O for a Thousand Tongues to Sing" and "Love Divine, All Loves Excelling."

GLORY be to God on high,
And Peace on Earth descend:
God comes down: He bows the Sky:
    He shows himself our Friend!
God th'Invisible *appears*,
    God the Blest, the Great I AM
Sojourns in this Vale of Tears,
    And JESUS is his Name.

Him the Angels all ador'd
    Their Maker and their King:
Tidings of their Humbled LORD
    They now to Mortals bring:
Emptied of his Majesty,
    Of His dazzling Glories shorn,
Beings Source *begins to* BE
    And GOD himself is BORN!

See th'Eternal Son of GOD
    A Mortal Son of Man,
Dwelling in an Earthly Clod
    Whom Heaven cannot contain!
Stand amaz'd ye Heavens at This!
    See the LORD of Earth and Skies
Humbled to the Dust He is,
    And in a Manger lies!

We the Sons of Men rejoice,
    The Prince of Peace proclaim,
With Heaven's Host lift up our Voice,
    And shout *Immanuel's* Name;
Knees and Hearts to Him we bow;
    Of our Flesh, and of our Bone
JESUS is our Brother now,
    And GOD is All our own!

Born of the Father's Heart

Spanish-born lawyer and civil servant Marcus Prudentius (348–413) is better known for his Latin Christian poetry. After entering a monastery, he wrote liturgical poems for the early Spanish Mozarabic rites.

BORN of the Father's heart
    Before the creation of the world,
Alpha and Omega named,
    Beginning and End of all that is,
He commanded and they were made,
    He spoke and they were fashioned:
Earth, heavens, the ocean depths,
    The three-fold spheres of the universe
And all that dwell in them
    Under the lofty sun and moon.
He took upon Himself the shape of man
    Limbs subject to the thrall of death,
That the seed of Adam might not perish
    Whom the dreadful law had plunged
Into the depths of Tartarus.
    O blessed that sacred birth!—
When the child-bearing Virgin
    Having conceived of the Holy Spirit,
Brought forth our salvation,
    And the Child, Redeemer of the world,
Revealed His sacred countenance.
    Sing, O vast heights of the heavens!
Sing, Angels, all powers that be!
    Sing, prophets, as you once foretold!
Let all things join in praising Him!
    Old men and young, choirs of children,
Mothers, virgins, infant girls,
    Praise Him with harmonious voices;
Let the turbulent rivers praise
    And the thunderous shores of the sea,
The storms and rain, the summer heat,
    Frost, snow, the forest breeze,
Day and night, let all unite,
    All celebrate His glory for evermore.

My mouth will utter the praise . . .

The greatest of early Christian theologians, Saint Augustine (354–430) began life in North Africa as a pagan, like his father. His beloved and devout Catholic mother, Saint Monnica, lived to see both her husband and her son converted. This selection, "Sermo in Natale Domini IV," was given after he became a priest in 391 C.E.

MY mouth will utter the praise of the Lord,
of the Lord through whom all things have been made
And who has been made amidst all things;

Who is the Revealer of His Father, Creator of His mother;
who is the Son of God from His Father without a mother,
The Son of Man through His mother without a father.

He is as great as the Day of the Angels,
and as small as a day in the life of men;
He is the Word of God before all ages,
and the Word made flesh at the destined time.

Maker of the sun, He is made beneath the sun.
Disposing all the ages from the bosom of the Father,
He consecrates this very day in the womb of His mother.
In His Father He abides; from His mother He goes forth.

Creator of heaven and earth,
under the heavens He was born upon earth.
Wise beyond all speech, as a speechless child He is wise.
Filling the whole world, He lies in a manger.
Ruling the stars, He nurses at His mother's breast.

He is great in the form of God
and small in the form of a servant,
So much so that His greatness
is not diminished by His smallness,
Nor His smallness concealed by His greatness.

For when He assumed a human body,
He did not forsake divine works.
He did not cease to be concerned mightily
from one end of the universe to the other,
And to order all things delightfully, when,
having clothed Himself in the fragility of the flesh,

He was received into, not confined in,
    the Virgin's womb.

So that, while the food of wisdom
    was not taken away from the angels,
We were to taste how sweet is the Lord.

Hosanna to Christ

Isaac Watts (1674–1748), the father of English hymnody, wrote more than six hundred hymns in his time. They include "Joy to the World," "Jesus Shall Reign Where'er the Sun," and "O God, Our Help in Ages Past."

HOSANNA to the royal son
Of David's ancient line!
His natures two, his person one,
    Mysterious and divine.

The root of David, here we find,
    And offspring, are the same:
Eternity and time are joined
    In our Immanuel's name.

Blest he that comes to wretched man
    With peaceful news from Heaven!
Hosannas, of the highest strain,
    To Christ the Lord be given.

Let mortals ne'er refuse to take
    The Hosanna on their tongues,
Lest rocks and stones should rise and break
    Their silence into songs.

Sound Over All Waters

Of Puritan and Quaker descent in Massachusetts, John Greenleaf Whittier (1807–1892) became an author and an abolitionist. He was editor of the New England Weekly Review *in Hartford, and he later became the most important writer of the abolitionist movement.*

SOUND over all waters, reach out from all lands,
The chorus of voices, the clasping of hands;
Sing hymns that were sung by the stars of the morn,
Sing songs of the angels when Jesus was born!
　　With glad jubilations
　　Bring hope to the nations!
The dark night is ending and dawn has begun:
Rise, hope of the ages, arise like the sun,
　　All speech flow to music, all hearts beat as one!

Sing the bridal of nations! with chorals of love;
Sing out the war-vulture and sing in the dove,
Till the hearts of the people keep time in accord,
And the voice of the world is the voice of the Lord!
　　Clasp hands of the nations
　　In strong gratulations:
The dark night is ending and dawn has begun;
Rise, hope of the ages, arise like the sun.
　　All speech flow to music, all hearts beat as one!

Blow bugles of battle, the marches of peace;
East, west, north and south, let the long quarrel cease:
Sing the song of great joy that the angels began,
Sing of glory to God and of good-will to man!
　　Hark, joining in chorus
　　The heavens bend o'er us!
The dark night is ending and dawn has begun:
Rise, hope of all ages, arise like the sun,
　　All speech flow to music, all hearts beat as one!

Such music . . .

For much of his life, John Milton (1608–1674) was a passionate Puritan and a follower of Cromwell against the monarchy in England. He retired in seclusion to write Paradise Lost *and other great works, enlisting the help of his talented daughter when he became blind. This selection is an excerpt from "Hymn on the Morning of Christ's Nativity," which has twenty-seven verses in all.*

SUCH music (as 'tis said)
Before was never made,
   But when of old the sons of morning sung,
While the Creator great
His constellations set,
   And the well-balanced world on hinges hung,
And cast the dark foundations deep,
And bid the weltering waves their oozy channels keep.

Ring out, ye crystal spheres!
Once bless our human ears
   (If ye have power to touch our senses so),
And let your silver chime
Move in melodious time;
   And let the bass of heaven's deep organ blow;
And with your ninefold harmony
Make up full consort to the angelic symphony.

For if such holy song
Enwrap our fancy long,
   Time will run back and fetch the age of gold;
And speckled Vanity
Will sicken soon and die,
   And leprous Sin will melt from earthly mould;
And Hell itself will pass away,
And leave her dolorous mansions to the peering day.

Yes, Truth and Justice then
Will down return to men,
   Orbed in a rainbow; and, like glories wearing,
Mercy will sit between,
Throned in celestial sheen,
   With radiant feet the tissued clouds down steering;
And Heaven, as at some festival,
Will open wide the gates of her high Palace Hall.

If Ye Would Hear the Angels Sing

A poet and hymn writer, Dora Greenwell (1821–1882) is the author of the collection A Present Heaven, *written in 1862.*

IF ye would hear the angels sing
    "Peace on earth and mercy mild,"
    Think of him who was once a child,
On Christmas Day in the morning.

If ye would hear the angels sing,
    Rise, and spread your Christmas fare;
    'Tis merrier still the more that share,
On Christmas Day in the morning.

Rise, and bake your Christmas bread:
    Christians, rise! the world is bare,
    And blank, and dark with want and care,
Yet Christmas comes in the morning.

If ye would hear the angels sing,
    Rise, and light your Christmas fire;
    And see that ye pile the logs still higher
On Christmas Day in the morning.

Rise, and light your Christmas fire;
    Christians, rise! the world is old,
    And Time is weary, and worn, and cold,
Yet Christmas comes in the morning.

If ye would hear the angels sing,
    Christians! see ye let each door
    Stand wider than it e'er stood before,
On Christmas Day in the morning.

Rise, and open wide the door;
    Christians, rise! the world is wide,
    And many there be that stand outside,
Yet Christmas comes in the morning.

From "Hymn in the Holy Nativity"

Raised a Puritan in England, the metaphysical poet Richard Crashaw (ca. 1613–1649) became a Roman Catholic shortly before his death. This selection is an excerpt from the eighteen original stanzas of his "Hymn in the Holy Nativity," which he wrote in 1648.

GLOOMY night embraced the place
Where the noble infant lay—
The babe looked up and shewed his face,
In spite of darkness it was day!
It was thy day, Sweet, and did rise,
Not from the East, but from thine eyes.

Winter chid aloud, and sent
The angry North to wage his wars.
The North forgot his fierce intent,
And left perfumes, instead of scars.
By those sweet eyes' persuasive powers
Where he meant frost, he scattered flowers.

We saw thee in thy balmy nest,
Bright dawn of our eternal day!
We saw thine eyes break from their East
And chase the trembling shades away;
We saw thee, and we blessed the sight;
We saw thee by thine own sweet light.

Welcome, all wonder in one sight,
Eternity shut in a span,
Summer in winter, day in night,
Heaven in earth, and God in man!
Great little one! whose all-embracing birth
Lifts earth to heaven, stoops heaven to earth.

Welcome; though not to gold nor silk,
To more than Caesar's birthright is;
Two sister seas of virgin-milk,
With many a rarely temper'd kiss,
That breathes at once both maid and mother,
Warms in the one, cools in the other.

Welcome, though not to those gay flies
Gilded i' th' beams of earthly kings,
Slippery souls in smiling eyes;
But to poor shepherds, homespun things,
Whose wealth's their flock, whose wit, to be
Well read in their simplicity.

Yet when young April's husband-show'rs
Shall bless the fruitful Maia's bed,
We'll bring the first-born of her flow'rs
To kiss thy feet and crown thy head.
To thee, dread Lamb! whose love must keep
The shepherds more than they the sheep.

To thee, meek Majesty! soft King
Of simple graces and sweet loves,
Each of us his lamb will bring,
Each his pair of silver doves;
Till burnt at last in fire of thy fair eyes,
Ourselves become our own best sacrifice.

The Mystic's Christmas

After working as a journalist and an editor in New England, John Greenleaf Whittier (1807–1892) upheld his Quaker ideals by becoming a passionate crusader against slavery. In later life he returned to literature and published several volumes of poetry and prose.

"ALL hail!" the bells of Christmas rang,
"All hail!" the monks at Christmas sang,
The merry monks who kept with cheer
The gladdest day of all their year.

But still apart, unmoved thereat,
A pious elder brother sat
Silent, in his accustomed place,
With God's sweet peace upon his face.

"Why sitt'st thou thus?" his brethren cried.
"It is the blessed Christmas-tide;
The Christmas lights are aglow,
The sacred lilies bud and blow.

"Above our heads the joy-bells ring,
Without the happy children sing,
And all God's creatures hail the morn
On which the holy Christ was born!

"Rejoice with us; no more rebuke
Our gladness with thy quiet look."
The gray monk answered: "Keep, I pray,
Even as ye list, the Lord's birthday.

"Let heathen Yule fires flicker red
Where thronged refectory feasts are spread;
With mystery-play and masque and mime
And wait-songs speed the holy time!

"The blindest faith may haply save;
The Lord accepts the things we have;
And reverence, howso'er it strays,
May find at last the shining ways.

"They needs must grope who cannot see,
The blade before the ear must be;
As ye are feeling I have felt,
And where ye dwell I too have dwelt.

"But now, beyond the things of sense,
Beyond occasions and events,
I know, through God's exceeding grace,
Release from form and time and place.

"I listen, from no mortal tongue,
To hear the song the angels sung;
And wait within myself to know
The Christmas lilies bud and blow.

"The outward symbols disappear
From his whose inward sight is clear;
And small must be the choice of days
To him who fills them all with praise!

"Keep while you need it, brothers mine,
With honest zeal your Christmas sign,
But judge not him who every morn
Feels in his heart the Lord Christ born!"

Index by Author

Acknowledgments (continued)

The editor gratefully acknowledges permission to reproduce the following copyrighted material:

Scriptural quotations in this book, unless otherwise noted, are from the New Revised Standard Version (NRSV) of the Bible. Copyright © 1989 by the Division of Christian Education of the National Council of Churches of Christ in the United States of America. All rights reserved.

W. H. Auden: From *W. H. Auden: Collected Poems*, by W. H. Auden, edited by Edward Mendelson. Copyright © 1944 and renewed 1972 by W. H. Auden. Reprinted by permission of Random House, Inc. and Faber and Faber Ltd.

Russell Baker: Column entitled "One of the Best," 18 December 1993. Copyright © 1993 by the New York Times Company. Reprinted by permission.

Byzantine prayer: A prayer from the Great Church of Constantinople, excerpted with permission from *Byzantine Daily Worship*, Allendale, NJ 07401.

Dom Helder Camara: "In the Middle of the Night," from *It's Midnight, Lord,* by Dom Helder Camara, translated by Joseph Gallagher, Thomas Fuller, and Tom Conry. Copyright © 1984; Washington, DC: Pastoral Press. Reprinted by permission.

Sor Juana Inés de la Cruz: "Carol #3," by Sor Juana Inés de la Cruz, from *The Roads from Bethlehem*. Copyright © 1993 by Pegram Johnson III and Edna M. Troiano. Used by permission of Westminster/John Knox Press.

Percy Dearmer: Extract from the preface by Percy Dearmer from *The Oxford Book of Carols*. Copyright © 1928 by Oxford Press.

Ruth Duck: "O Radiant Christ, Incarnate Word," by Ruth Duck. Used by permission of G. I. A. Publications, Inc., Chicago, IL, exclusive agent. All rights reserved.

Padraic Fallon: "Mater Dei," from *Poems,* by Padraic Fallon. Copyright © 1974 by Dolmen Press. Reprinted by permission of Carcanet Press Ltd.

Lawrence Ferlinghetti: "Christ Climbed Down," from *A Coney Island of the Mind,* by Lawrence Ferlinghetti. Copyright © 1958 by Lawrence Ferlinghetti. Reprinted by permission of New Directions Publishing Corp.